The Technopolitics

Navigating the Intersection of Technology and Politics in the Digital Age

Rahul Pawar & Ishwar Singh

ISBN 978-93-5667-862-0
© Rahul Pawar & Ishwar Singh 2023

Published in India 2023 by Pencil

Contributors:
Co-Author: Birinder Pal Kaur
Co-Author: Kanchan Pawar

A brand of
One Point Six Technologies Pvt. Ltd.
Unit no. 26, Ground Floor, Building A1,
Wadala Truck Terminal Road,
Near Post Office, Antop Hill, Mumbai - 400037
E connect@thepencilapp.com
W www.thepencilapp.com

Author biography

Throughout his career, Ishwar has published numerous influential papers and authored several books on political theory, comparative politics, and public policy. His research has shed light on issues such as democratic governance, political ideologies, social movements, and the impact of globalization on politics. His insightful analysis and ability to connect theoretical frameworks with real-world phenomena have earned him acclaim within the academic community.

Ishwar Singh's contributions to the field of political science have been widely recognized. He has received numerous accolades and awards for his outstanding research and teaching. His work has not only advanced the academic understanding of political science but has also influenced policymakers and practitioners in their decision-making processes.

After completing his formal education, Rahul embarked on a career as a computer scientist, dedicating himself to research and development. He joined a prominent technology company, where he worked on cutting-edge projects that pushed the boundaries of innovation. Rahul's expertise in machine learning and artificial intelligence allowed him to make significant breakthroughs in the development of intelligent systems and algorithms.

Rahul has published numerous research papers in esteemed journals, sharing his findings and advancements with the scientific community. His work has focused on leveraging machine learning techniques to solve complex problems, improve decision-making processes, and enhance the efficiency of systems.

CONTENTS

Epigraph

"The advent of the digital age has ushered in a new era of possibilities, when politics and technology are now more intricately intertwined than ever before. We are situated in this dynamic environment, where we must contend with both the dangers of power and the promise of development. Let's keep in mind as we go through this environment that our decisions affect the future and that it is our common duty to make sure that technology meets the needs of all people.

Foreword

It is becoming more and more obvious that the convergence of technology and politics is a crucial area that requires our attention at a time when technology dominates society and digital improvements pervade every aspect of our lives. A new age has begun as a result of the quick advancement of technology, which has had an impact on our society, economy, and even the fundamental nature of the human experience. In light of this, "The Technopolitics: Navigating the Intersection of Technology and Politics in the Digital Age" stands out as an insightful examination of the nuanced interactions between politics and technology.

This book, written by great brains and committed thinkers, offers a thorough analysis of the complex forces at work in the field of technopolitics. It explores the substantial effects of technology on political systems, governance structures, and social norms, posing important queries about the relationships between power and authority, moral issues, and the direction this interconnected field may take in the future.

Understanding the fundamental significance and possible consequences of emerging transformational technologies like artificial intelligence, big data, blockchain, and many others is crucial. Technopolitics emerges as the crucial prism through which we may make sense of this constantly changing environment, appreciate its complexities, and predict its course in the future.

By compellingly examining the social, economic, and political effects of technology, "The Technopolitics" challenges our understanding of the paradigms and presumptions that underlie our modern digital world. It urges policymakers, inventors, and citizens to actively engage in defining the technopolitical environment for the benefit of society as a whole while challenging us to tackle the ethical quandaries emerging from the use and misuse of technology.

This book's chapters cover a broad variety of subjects, including the influence of social media on political discourse, the promise of technology to encourage civic involvement, the negative effects of monitoring, and the increasing role of algorithms in decision-making. In order to provide a comprehensive understanding of the topic, it covers a wide variety of viewpoints and draws on the expertise of academics, professionals, and thought leaders from numerous fields.

The book "The Technopolitics" gives more than just a theoretical analysis of the topic; it also makes useful suggestions. We can fight to create a more equal, open, and inclusive future by comprehending the complex interactions between politics and technology. This book is a call to action for people, groups, and governments to engage critically with the possibilities and problems the digital era presents while defending our democratic principles and basic rights.

As we set out on our voyage into the world of technopolitics, let us embrace technology's revolutionary potential while steadfastly upholding the principles that make us who we are as people. The future is in our hands, and "The Technopolitics" is our road map, enabling us to successfully negotiate the constantly shifting terrain of the digital era.

Together, let's explore the complicated landscape where politics and technology meet since it is here that our common future will take shape.

Birinder Pal Kaur

Preface

Modern society has undergone a profound transformation as a result of the quick development of technology, which has changed the way we live, work, and govern ourselves. An unprecedented degree of interconnection has been brought about by the digital revolution, providing people and countries with new tools and opportunities. But with this extraordinary development comes the urgent need to critically assess the complex link between politics and technology—a relationship that we either ignore or are unable to completely appreciate.

This convergence is explored in "The Technopolitics: Navigating the Intersection of Technology and Politics in the Digital Age," a trip into the center of a dynamic and changing terrain where the worlds of technology and politics collide. We explore the intricate interaction between technology advancements, social dynamics, and political institutions in this book in an effort to highlight the difficulties and possibilities that derive from it.

This book is the result of my own experiences navigating the complex landscape of the digital era as well as my own in-depth study, analysis, and conversations with professionals from a variety of professions. It is aimed at decision-makers, academics, technologists, activists, and curious minds who understand the importance of understanding how technology is having a profound impact on our political systems and the need to influence that trajectory in a way that is consistent with our shared goals and values.

In "The Technopolitics," we set out on a multifaceted investigation that takes into account numerous aspects of this complex connection. We investigate how social media sites and algorithmic systems affect political discourse and democratic procedures, explore the complexities of privacy and surveillance in a society that is becoming more and more interconnected, and explore the moral questions raised by cutting-edge technologies like artificial intelligence and biotechnology.

This book also explores the role of technology in political action and mobilization, emphasizing the transformational potential of digital technologies to create social movements and subvert existing hierarchies of power. We probe the need for accountable governance to promote the fair distribution of benefits and reduce possible hazards as we examine the delicate balance between technology innovation and regulatory frameworks.

"The Technopolitics" does not claim to provide conclusive solutions or answers to the complicated problems we confront. Instead, it acts as a manual, providing a thorough framework and a deep knowledge of how politics and technology interact. It promotes discussion, stimulates critical thinking, and gives people the tools they need to make informed and independent decisions in an ever-changing environment.

As we begin this inquiry, it is crucial to understand that the decisions we make now will affect how our societies develop in the future and how our democratic institutions are constructed as a whole. Technology and politics' interaction is a field that requires participation from all parties involved and is not just for professionals. We can actively contribute in directing our technology future and ensuring that it reflects our shared ideals of justice, equality, and human flourishing by comprehending the underlying forces at play.

Let's set out on this intellectual journey together because only by working together will we be able to navigate the tension between politics and technology in the digital age and create a future that harnesses technology's transformative potential while preserving the values that underpin our societies.

Rahul Pawar & Ishwar Singh

Acknowledgements

We would like to express our sincere gratitude and appreciation to our beloved parents, Smt. Amarjit Kaur, Shri Pal Singh, Smt. Saroj Pawar, and Shri Tilak Pawar, for their unfailing support, love, and encouragement during our journey to research and write this thesis on "Pixels and Politicians: Examining the Impact of Computer Science on Political Campaigns." Our success has been greatly aided by their advice and support, and we will always be grateful to them for their tremendous efforts.

First and foremost, we want to express our gratitude to Smt. Amarjit Kaur and Smt. Saroj Pawar, our moms. Our lives have been supported by their love and sacrifice. They have consistently served as our pillars of support, inspiration, and comprehension. Our ability to overcome obstacles and achieve our academic goals has been fueled by their unwavering support and faith in our skills.

We owe a debt of appreciation to our dads, Shri Pal Singh and Shri Tilak Pawar, for their priceless advice and knowledge. They have continuously served as an inspiration to us, showing us the value of tenacity, diligence, and commitment. Our paths and aspirations have been significantly shaped and nurtured by their constant support and faith in our goals.

We also want to express our gratitude to our parents for giving up things in order to provide us the greatest educational opportunity. To make sure we had access to high-quality education and resources, they worked diligently and even made personal sacrifices. Our strong feeling of appreciation and desire to live up to their standards have been inspired by their selflessness and devotion.

We are appreciative of our parents for creating a culture that values education and curiosity. They fostered our intellectual development from an early age, motivating us to look into new concepts, challenge the existing quo, and become passionate about learning. Their unshakable faith in the value of education has helped to mold us into critical thinkers and lifelong learners.

Additionally, we would want to express our sincere gratitude for the many sacrifices our parents have made in order to provide for us materially, morally, and emotionally. They have always been our pillars of support, providing direction in trying times and exulting in our victories as no one else can. Their unshakable faith in our competence has given us the courage to follow our aspirations bravely.

We also want to thank our parents for their incredible tolerance and understanding during this process. They have given advice, been a listening ear, and given the emotional support required to go through the highs and lows of academic research. Even in our self-doubt, their confidence in us has been a tremendous source of support.

We also like to thank our parents for their support and interest in our academic endeavors. Our research interests have been significantly shaped by their constant encouragement to investigate new areas, participate in thought-provoking debates, and pursue greatness. Our enthusiasm for examining how computer science affects political campaigns has been stoked by their faith in the ability of education to bring about good change.

For their incalculable contributions to our life and this thesis, our parents, Smt. Amarjit Kaur, Shri Pal Singh, Smt. Saroj Pawar, and Shri Tilak Pawar, deserve the deepest gratitude. This scientific project would not have been feasible without their unfailing support, love, and advice. They have been a continual source of inspiration and strength in our lives. We dedicate this thesis to our parents in appreciation of the tireless work they did to mold us into the people we are today. May we always strive to honor them in whatever we do.

The Technopolitics

Chapter 1

Introduction

The term "technopolitics" refers to the study of the complex interrelationship between politics and technology. It refers to the effect of political choices and ideas on the creation and use of technology as well as the impact of technical breakthroughs on political institutions, structures, and processes. In the current day, technology has permeated every area of our lives and changed the way we govern ourselves, connect with others, and communicate with one another. As a result, technology has also had a significant influence on politics and power relationships, influencing societies and changing the parameters of government.

Technopolitics covers a wide variety of topics, including how technology affects activism, government, surveillance, and political communication. The evolution of communication channels is one of technology's most noticeable impacts on politics. Increased access to information, the ability to organize large-scale movements, and the development of new types of political involvement and participation have all been made possible by the emergence of the internet and social media platforms. Bypassing conventional information gatekeepers has made it possible for people to quickly communicate ideas and support the development of internet groups devoted to certain political objectives.

Technopolitics has also influenced the development of fresh types of political activity. Online forums provide people a place to air their complaints, plan demonstrations, and promote social and political change. Digital technologies have been used by movements like the Arab Spring, Occupy Wall Street, and Black Lives Matter to organize followers, plan events, and magnify their ideas. Technology has given citizens and disenfranchised groups the capacity to question established power systems, call for accountability, and demand legislative changes.

Politics and technology colliding, however, also brings up issues with privacy, monitoring, and the consolidation of power. Governments and businesses use technology to monitor individuals' internet activity, gather personal information, and impose control over information flows. Discussions on civil liberties, privacy rights, and the moral implications of technical progress have been spurred by this. Big data gathering and usage by political campaigns and governments have sparked concerns about the possibility of algorithmic bias, the swaying of public opinion, and the degradation of democratic processes.

Technopolitics also touches on other important topics including cybersecurity, automation, artificial intelligence, and the digital divide. In order to secure key networks and infrastructure from cyber attacks, it is necessary to implement strong security measures due to the growing dependence on digital infrastructure and linked systems. The emergence of automation and artificial intelligence has substantial effects on job displacement, socioeconomic inequality, and labor markets, sparking discussions on the need for policies to promote fair results in the face of fast technological change. The digital gap also draws attention to differences in access to technology, information, and digital literacy that may aggravate already-existing social and economic inequities.

The intricate interaction between politics and technology that affects and shapes numerous facets of our society is referred to as technopolitics. Political activity, communication, governance, and power relations have all changed as a result, opening up new avenues for involvement and participation but also bringing up issues with privacy, surveillance, and the concentration of power. In order to guarantee that the advantages of technology be tapped while reducing the possible hazards and pitfalls, critical analysis, ethical considerations, and proactive policy responses will need to be made. The continual improvements in technology will continue to transform the political environment. A developing subject of study, technopolitics aims to comprehend and negotiate the complex interplay between politics and technology in the information era.

Chapter 2

The Rise of Technopolitics

2. Introduction

With the advent of the digital age, politics throughout the world have seen a significant upheaval in recent decades. The conventional political environment has undergone a radical upheaval known as technopolitics, which has altered power relationships, public participation, and policy-making procedures. The field of "technopolitics" refers to the nexus between politics and technology, where the tools and developments of the digital age are used to influence and affect political discourse, government, and decision-making.

The quick development of information and communication technologies (ICTs) is one of the main factors contributing to the advent of technopolitics. The widespread use of social media, cellphones, and the internet has significantly altered how individuals obtain and exchange information. Citizens now have more power thanks to the democratization of information, making it possible for them to participate in politics more actively and with more knowledge. The conventional limitations of time and geography have been overcome by the digital sphere as a platform for political discourse, activity, and mobilization.

Particularly social media platforms have been crucial to the development of technopolitics. These platforms offer a virtual public realm where people may express their thoughts, talk about current events, and plan mass actions. Bypassing traditional media gatekeepers and establishing direct communication channels with the audience, political campaigns and movements are increasingly using social media to connect with and organize followers. With social media acting as a forum for citizen journalism and examination of political elites, the power relations between politicians, citizens, and media companies have changed.

Additionally, the nature of political engagement has changed as a result of technopolitics. Citizens may now participate in politics in a variety of ways beyond the traditional ones, such as voting and attending public events. Online platforms have created new opportunities for involvement, including crowdsourcing of policy ideas, online consultations, and e-petitions. Through digital platforms, people may communicate with their elected officials directly, sharing their opinions and influencing how policies are made. Political processes may become more inclusive and open to all people, which would improve democratic governance and close the communication gap between the people and their representatives.

Election and campaign procedures have seen substantial modifications as a result of technology in politics. Political actors may customize their messaging and campaign methods to target particular demographic groups, enhancing their reach and influence. This is made possible by data analytics and targeting techniques. Online advertising and micro-targeting have developed into potent instruments for political persuasion, affecting voter behavior and forming public opinion. But in the age of technopolitics, worries about data privacy, the propagation of false information, and public opinion manipulation have also become significant problems, raising issues about the morality of using technology in political settings.

Technopolitics has transformed government and policy-making in addition to citizen participation and election campaigns. Data analytics, artificial intelligence (AI), and machine learning algorithms are being used by governments all over the world to help them make decisions and enhance service delivery. Smart cities are being created, leveraging networked technology to improve urban sustainability and efficiency. Citizens may now access public services online thanks to e-governance efforts, which also streamline administrative procedures and increase transparency. However, in the age of technopolitics, achieving fair and inclusive governance is difficult due to the digital gap and uneven access to technology.

Additionally, the emergence of technopolitics has affected both internal politics and foreign relations. In order to influence public opinion, interact with international audiences, and project their soft power, nations now use social media platforms and online forums known as "digital diplomacy." As state-sponsored hacking and misinformation efforts threaten national security and the legitimacy of democratic institutions, cybersecurity has become a crucial issue. Global internet governance and the regulation of cutting-edge technology are hotly contested issues that are the topic of international negotiations.

In conclusion, the emergence of technopolitics is indicative of a political revolution. Politics and technology have come together to change how authority is used, how individuals interact, and how policies are created and carried out. Political procedures and institutions have undergone a profound change as a result of the democratization of information, the empowerment of individuals through social media, and the digitalization of government. While there are many prospects for public involvement, openness, and efficiency offered by technopolitics, it also offers issues with privacy, false information, and inequity.

As a result of the fast development of information and communication technologies (ICTs) and the digital era, technopolitics has emerged and has undergone significant change in the political sphere. The world's power structures, public participation, and policy-making processes have all changed as a result of the convergence of technology and politics, which has fundamentally altered the old political landscape.

The democratization of information is one of the primary drivers of the growth of technopolitics. The growing use of cellphones, social networking sites, and the internet has significantly altered how individuals access, use, and exchange information. Citizens now actively participate in creating the political narrative rather than merely relying on traditional media channels for news and political dialogue. A more educated and involved populace has resulted from this empowerment since people may now access a wide range of perspectives and ideas from both mainstream and alternative sources.

Particularly social media platforms have been crucial to the development of technopolitics. These platforms offer a digital public space where people may express their thoughts, participate in political discourse, and plan mass actions. Bypassing traditional media gatekeepers and establishing direct communication channels with the audience, political campaigns and social movements increasingly use social media to connect with and organize followers. With social media platforms acting as a platform for citizen journalism, real-time information transmission, and public scrutiny of political elites, the power dynamics between politicians, citizens, and media outlets have changed.

Additionally, the nature of political engagement has changed as a result of technopolitics. Online platforms have created new opportunities for political engagement while still valuing more established ones like voting and attending public events. Citizens may now directly affect political decisions and policy results because to the growing popularity of e-petitions, online consultations, and crowdsourcing of policy ideas. By encouraging inclusion, openness, and citizen-led initiatives, the digital sphere has the potential to improve democratic government.

Election and campaign procedures have seen substantial modifications as a result of technology in politics. Political actors can focus their messaging and campaign plans to particular demographic groups to increase their reach and influence by using data analytics and targeted advertising approaches. Micro-targeting has developed into a potent instrument for political persuasion, affecting public opinion and voter behavior because to the massive volumes of data created through digital interactions. However, issues with data privacy, the dissemination of false information, and the swaying of public opinion have become serious problems in the age of technopolitics, raising concerns about the morality of using technology in political settings.

Technopolitics has transformed government and policy-making in addition to citizen participation and election campaigns. Governments all around the globe are using data analytics, artificial intelligence (AI), and machine learning algorithms to improve service delivery and inform decision-making. Smart cities are being created, utilizing networked technology to improve urban sustainability and efficiency. Citizens may now access public services online thanks to e-governance efforts, which also streamline administrative procedures and increase transparency. However, in the age of technopolitics, achieving fair and inclusive governance is difficult due to the digital gap and uneven access to technology.

Additionally, the emergence of technopolitics has affected both internal politics and foreign relations. The use of social media platforms, online forums, and digital networks by governments to influence public opinion, interact with foreign publics, and project their soft power has given rise to a new type of diplomatic engagement known as "digital diplomacy." As dangers to national security and the integrity of democratic processes such as state-sponsored hacking, misinformation campaigns, and the weaponization of information have grown, cybersecurity has become an urgent concern. Global internet governance and the regulation of cutting-edge technology are hotly contested issues that are the topic of international negotiations.

2.1 Defining Technopolitics

Technopolitics acknowledges that technology is not politically neutral; rather, it has political consequences by nature. It looks at the intricate relationships between technology advancements and the resulting social, economic, and political effects. This field of research examines how the dynamics of power, control, and resistance in connection to technology impact political and social structures.

Numerous subjects and problems are looked at in technopolitics, including:

- Digital governance: Digital governance is the use of digital platforms and technology to the governing process. It includes e-government efforts, digital democracy, and the effects of surveillance technologies on individual rights.

- Internet and Social Movements: How social media and the internet are used to mobilize and coordinate political movements, such as protests, uprisings, and online activism.

- Privacy and Surveillance: How technology improvements may affect how individuals' private information is collected and used by governments and businesses for surveillance purposes.

- Technological Determinism: The idea that technology is the primary force behind social and political development as well as an examination of its drawbacks and detractors.

- The study of risks and conflicts in the digital sphere, including problems with cyberattacks, information warfare, and the use of technology in national security.

- Digital Divide: The social and political ramifications of unequal access to and use of technology, as well as initiatives to close the gap between those who have access to it and those who do not.

- Ethical Implications: The analysis of moral conundrums caused by the creation and application of technology, such as AI ethics, algorithmic prejudice, and the accountability of tech corporations.

2.2 The Intersection of Technology and Politics

Modern society is now recognized for its convergence of politics and technology. Technology has a growing impact on political institutions, procedures, and governance as it continues to progress at an unparalleled rate. Technology has fundamentally changed the way politics is practiced, from the way campaigns are run to the way governments engage with their public.

The evolution of political communication is one of technology's most noticeable effects on politics. The emergence of social media and the internet has completely changed how individuals and politicians interact. Political figures may now communicate with their supporters directly via social media platforms, cutting out conventional media middlemen. A new kind of grassroots activity and political mobilization has resulted from this, allowing people to express their thoughts, start movements, and shape public opinion. However, it has also brought forth problems including the propagation of false information, the emergence of echo chambers, and the decline in confidence in conventional media sources.

Political processes now operate more effectively and transparently thanks in large part to technology. For instance, the use of electronic voting technologies has sped up election results while streamlining the process and reducing mistakes. Digital platforms have also improved the accessibility of public information, participation in policymaking, and the ability of voters to hold elected leaders responsible. In order to assess and monitor government operations, spot inefficiencies, and suggest data-driven remedies, individuals now have unparalleled access to government information thanks to open data programs. However, as governments amass enormous quantities of personal data, worries about privacy, data security, and the possibility for monitoring have also surfaced.

Technology has evolved into a potent weapon for political campaigns, in addition to communication and procedure improvements. Political parties increasingly often utilize data analytics, artificial intelligence, and machine learning algorithms to target voters, create tailored messaging, and improve campaign methods. With the use of these technology, campaigns are now able to analyze vast quantities of data, pinpoint voter preferences and habits, and modify their messaging to appeal to certain groups. But the use of these technologies has brought up moral concerns about invasion of privacy, manipulation, and the potential for political divisiveness.

Technology has also been helpful in encouraging political and civic involvement. People may now more easily obtain information about candidates, take part in debates, contribute to campaigns, and even run for office thanks to online and mobile platforms. Platforms for crowdsourcing have democratized financing, enabling underfunded challengers to go up against incumbents who have a lot of money. Digital technologies have also made it easier to plan protests, rallies, and social movements, giving voice to voices that might otherwise go unheard. But the digital gap, where certain groups lack access to or proficiency with technology, may aggravate already-existing disparities in political engagement.

Beyond domestic issues, international relations are also affected by the nexus of technology and politics. Governments are increasingly at risk from state-sponsored hacking, cyberwarfare, and misinformation efforts, therefore cybersecurity has become a major issue. Nations are now competing to build cutting-edge cyber defense and assault capabilities. Furthermore, difficult moral and legal issues have been brought up by the use of technology in monitoring, intelligence collection, and espionage. Governments are battling to strike the correct balance between defending individuals and upholding civil rights as the lines between personal privacy and national security have become hazy.

The political environment has undergone various changes as a result of the interaction of technology and politics. It has revolutionised political campaigns, encouraged public involvement, improved the efficiency and openness of political processes, and impacted international relations. Although technology provides many advantages, it has also created problems including the proliferation of false information, privacy issues, moral quandaries, and digital inequality. Policymakers and society at large must manage these issues as technology develops in order to fully use its promise while preserving democratic ideals and guaranteeing an inclusive and fair political system.

Additionally, the nexus between politics and technology has significantly influenced how policies are created and governments are run. Governments now have the ability to create targeted policies and make choices based on solid evidence thanks to big data analytics and predictive modeling. Policymakers may learn about social trends, economic patterns, and public mood by examining enormous volumes of data. This data-driven methodology enables more efficient resource allotment and policy actions. Governments might, for instance, employ data analysis to pinpoint crime hotspots and distribute resources appropriately, or they can use predictive modeling to foresee healthcare requirements and prepare the necessary infrastructure and resources. But the use of automated decision-making and dependence on algorithms raises questions about fairness, prejudice, and the potential to dehumanize government.

The development of e-governance has also been made possible by technology, changing the dynamic between governments and their constituents. People may now access government services, submit forms and applications, and communicate with government agencies more easily thanks to online platforms and digital services. As a result, administrative procedures have been simplified, bureaucracy has been decreased, and public service delivery has been more effective. Governments have also used technology to promote accountability and transparency. Citizens now have immediate access to government data, budgets, and spending thanks to open government programs like open budgets and web portals. Because of this, people can keep an eye on how their government is doing, spot corruption, and verify that public monies are being spent properly. E-governance projects, especially in vulnerable groups, may be less successful due to the digital gap and inequities in internet access.

Furthermore, cutting-edge innovations like blockchain have the potential to alter governmental processes like elections and public administration. Blockchain technology is well suited for applications like secure online voting or tamper-proof record-keeping because it provides improved security, transparency, and immutability. Governments may enhance the integrity of public data and raise voter confidence in voting processes by using decentralized and transparent technologies. However, scalability, user acceptance, and resolving possible vulnerabilities present difficulties for the deployment of such systems.

The usage of developing technologies also generates ethical and legal questions at the nexus of technology and politics. Automation and artificial intelligence (AI) have the potential to upend labor markets, which would result in job displacement and economic inequality. The ethical ramifications of implementing AI systems must be considered by governments, especially in domains like autonomous weaponry and face recognition. achieving the ideal balance between technical progress and moral principles It becomes essential to make sure that technology respects human rights and promotes the larger good.

Additionally, new difficulties for international relations have been brought about by technology's global nature. The lines between conventional diplomacy and digital platforms and social media networks have become hazy, allowing states and non-state entities to engage in information warfare, misinformation operations, and cyberwarfare. Governments and international organizations have difficult hurdles in attributing cyberattacks and creating global standards and laws in cyberspace. To combat cybersecurity threats, safeguard vital infrastructure, and set norms controlling state activity in cyberspace, cooperation is required.

2.3 Historical Context and Evolution

The introduction of computers and the internet, which transformed communication and information exchange, is where the historical setting and development of digital democracy can be tracked. Digital democracy has its origins in more general democratic movements and the aim to increase public engagement in decision-making. Direct democracy in ancient Athens gave way to representative democracies throughout history, and the development of modern technology has created new opportunities for public involvement and participation.

As the public's access to the internet increased in the latter half of the 20th century, the idea of digital democracy rose to prominence. Early on, information transmission and a few types of public interaction were the main uses of digital technology. However, the opportunity for wider engagement and interaction substantially grew with the emergence of social media platforms and online discussion boards.

The advent of e-government efforts in the late 1990s was the first significant example of digital democracy. Digital platforms are now being used by governments to provide online services and involve individuals in decision-making. People could now access government information and voice their thoughts online, which represented a huge change towards a more participatory democracy.

As the internet spread, digital democracy went beyond projects run by the government. Digital platforms have been used by grassroots movements and civil society groups to rally followers, spread awareness, and advance a range of causes. Online petitions, fundraising efforts, and social media activism have all become popular methods for encouraging individual and group engagement.

Early in the new millennium, platforms for collaboration and open-source software began to grow in popularity, further promoting public involvement and participation. Wikipedia and other similar initiatives have shown the value of group knowledge generation and the possibilities of decentralized decision-making. Digital democracy was built on the principle of harnessing the collective intellect of the people via technological means.

The widespread use of smartphones and the introduction of social media platforms have significantly advanced the development of digital democracy. People could participate in democratic processes whenever and wherever they wanted because to the continual connection and real-time information access offered by mobile devices. Platforms for social media like Facebook and

Twitter played a crucial role in promoting political discourse, organizing movements, and sharing information.

However, the emergence of social media has spawned fresh problems and worries. The quality of public debate was impacted, and democratic principles were undermined, by problems including false information, echo chambers, and algorithmic biases. The Cambridge Analytica affair and foreign meddling in elections brought to light the flaws and moral quandaries inherent in digital democracy.

In recent years, initiatives have been launched to solve these issues and change the face of digital democracy. Governments and internet firms have begun putting policies into place to counteract false information, increase transparency, and safeguard user privacy. For a better online environment for democratic dialogue, programs like fact-checking, content control, and algorithmic transparency have been implemented.

Additionally, cutting-edge innovations like blockchain and artificial intelligence have the potential to improve digital democracy. While AI-powered technologies may help in the analysis of massive volumes of data and the provision of individualized civic information to voters, blockchain technology provides possible answers for safe and transparent voting systems.

Future technical and sociological improvements are expected to continue to influence how digital democracy develops. The difficulties and possibilities related to digital democracy will continue to exist as digital technology are more incorporated into our daily lives. To secure a dynamic and inclusive digital democracy for the future, it will be crucial to find a balance between technical innovation, democratic principles, and the preservation of individual rights.

The development of digital democracy in recent years has been characterized by a number of noteworthy trends and difficulties. The rise of online debating forums and participatory budgeting efforts is one noticeable trend. These platforms provide chances for people to participate in insightful debates, work together on policy ideas, and actively affect decision-making procedures. Online discussion allows people who may not have previously participated in political processes to express their thoughts and influence the creation of public policy. This is a more accessible and inclusive kind of democracy.

The employment of data-driven initiatives in digital democracy is a noteworthy development as well. Governments and organizations may use insights from big data and advanced analytics to better understand the preferences, habits, and requirements of their constituents. This information may help in the development of evidence-based policy and allow more specialized and adaptable public services. While concerns of privacy, permission, and algorithmic bias must be carefully addressed to ensure that data-driven initiatives are fair and inclusive, the ethical use of data in digital democracy continues to be a major concern.

The proliferation of false information and disinformation is among the main obstacles to the development of digital democracy. Because it is so simple to share information on digital platforms, incorrect or misleading material may spread quickly, possibly affecting public opinion and distorting democratic processes. In order to address this issue and stop the spread of false information without restricting free speech, a multifaceted strategy incorporating media literacy training, fact-checking programs, and responsible platform administration is needed.

A major obstacle to the development of digital democracy is the problem of digital inequality. The digital gap restricts access and makes it difficult for underprivileged people to participate fully, even while digital technologies have the potential to increase citizen involvement. By boosting digital literacy initiatives, extending internet access, and ensuring that technical infrastructure is inclusive and available to everyone, efforts must be taken to close the gap.

The impact of social media algorithms and filter bubbles on democratic debate is another problem. Social media sites often utilize algorithms to prioritize material based on users' past actions and preferences, resulting in echo chambers where people are mostly exposed to views that align with their own. As a result, there may be more polarization, less exposure to opposing ideas, and fragmentation of the public dialogue. It is a challenging endeavor that needs continual study and regulation to create algorithms that support varied content and foster free discussion while respecting user choices and privacy.

Last but not least, it is crucial to address the problem of internet security and defend democratic processes from cyberthreats. To preserve the credibility and validity of digital democracy, it is essential to handle the difficulties of ensuring the integrity of digital voting systems, preventing hacking efforts, and defending against outside meddling in elections.

Despite these obstacles, the development of digital democracy still has a lot of promise to promote participation by citizens, inclusion, and transparency in decision-making. Societies may use the potential of digital democracy to create more robust, participatory democracies in the future by embracing technical breakthroughs, addressing related dangers, and preserving democratic ideals.

Chapter 3

Technological Advancements and Society

3. Introduction

The development of technology has had a huge influence on society, changing many facets of our lives and causing important shifts throughout the world. The fast advancement of technology over the last several decades has changed the way we interact, study, work, and amuse ourselves. These technological developments, which range from the development of the internet and the widespread use of smartphones to the emergence of automation and artificial intelligence (AI), have benefited society while also posing problems.

The revolution in communication that technology has sparked is among the biggest shifts. People from all around the globe are now linked through the internet, allowing for easy contact and teamwork. Platforms for social networking, information sharing, and community mobilization have become significant tools. This increased connectedness has made it easier to share information and viewpoints, promoting a worldwide flow of knowledge. It has, however, also raised issues with privacy, false information, and the dissemination of hate speech.

The workplace has undergone a change thanks to technology. Processes have been simplified, productivity has grown, and industries have been altered by automation and AI. Now that routine operations can be automated, human employees are free to concentrate on more challenging and innovative projects. But this has sparked worries about job loss and a possible rise in economic inequality. A continual process of learning and adaptation is required for both people and society as a whole as a result of the change to a digital economy, which has increased the need for new skills and abilities.

Technology has had a big impact on education as well. Digital resources and online learning platforms have increased educational accessibility by enabling people to study at their own speed and convenience. Through the use of immersive educational experiences, virtual reality and augmented reality technology have improved experiential learning. However, since not everyone has access to technology or the knowledge necessary to use it effectively, the digital divide continues to be a problem.

Technology has made significant improvements in the healthcare industry. Diagnoses, treatments, and patient monitoring have been transformed by advances in medical imaging, telemedicine, and wearable technology. Large datasets can now be analyzed to find patterns and make precise predictions using data analytics and machine learning algorithms. This has paved the way for customized medicine and more potent therapies. However, there is ongoing discussion over the moral implications of data privacy, security, and the ethical use of AI in healthcare.

The entertainment sector has also changed as a result of technology. Streaming services, which provide on-demand access to a variety of material, have upended conventional media consumption habits. Immersive games and interactive experiences are becoming more feasible thanks to virtual reality and augmented reality. The dynamics of fame and notoriety have changed as a result of social media influencers and content providers. However, issues like addiction, privacy, and the negative effects of too much screen time on mental health have come up.

There have been substantial improvements in transportation as well. Urban transportation might undergo a revolution as a result of the development of electric cars, automated driving systems, and ride-sharing services, which could also increase safety. However, for these technologies to be widely used, infrastructural development, legal frameworks, and ethical considerations are necessary. For instance, self-driving cars must be programmed to make judgments in potentially life-threatening scenarios.

Transactions are now quicker, more secure, and more convenient thanks to the development of digital payment methods like mobile wallets and cryptocurrencies. E-commerce platforms have created new channels for companies to access international markets, changing the retail environment and customer habits. Thoughts about cybersecurity, fraud, and data breaches have also grown as a result of the increased dependence on digital transactions, underscoring the need for strong security precautions and user education.

It is impossible to ignore how technology is affecting government and public services. Governments all across the globe are using technology to improve public service delivery, increase transparency, and encourage citizen involvement. Initiatives in e-governance have reduced administrative procedures, cutting down on corruption and inefficiency. Interconnected systems and data analytics are being used in "smart cities" to optimize resource management, boost public safety, and increase quality of life. Huge quantities of data are being gathered and used, but this raises issues with privacy, monitoring, and possible abuse.

The development of technology has also altered social interactions and relationships. Platforms for social media have spread widely, allowing users to communicate, share experiences, and participate in online communities. However, worries have been expressed over social media's effects on mental health, self-esteem, and the dissemination of false information. There have been talks about digital etiquette, cyberbullying, and the necessity for digital literacy as a result of the blurring of the lines between the real world and the virtual one.

In addition, technology has been instrumental in tackling global issues and advancing sustainability initiatives. Technologies for producing renewable energy, including solar and wind power, are gaining popularity because they provide alternatives to fossil fuels and cut down on carbon emissions. Devices and sensors from the IoT (Internet of Things) are being used to monitor and manage resources, improve energy efficiency, and promote environmental preservation. However, the quick rate of technical development also increases electronic waste and raises concerns about the long-term effects of technological innovation on the environment.

The main topic of conversation when it comes to technical breakthroughs and society is ethics. For instance, prejudice, accountability, and openness must be carefully considered in the creation and usage of AI. We must continue to monitor and regulate algorithmic decision-making since it has the potential to exacerbate current societal injustices. To guarantee that people have control over and knowledge of how their personal information is used, discussions on data privacy and consent are essential.

The development of technology has had a significant influence on many elements of life, presenting both possibilities and difficulties. Technology has changed communication, employment, education, healthcare, entertainment, transportation, economics, government, and social relationships because of its interconnection and accessibility. The ethical, social, and environmental repercussions of these developments must be carefully considered, however. To fully use technology while minimizing its negative effects, society must actively participate in debates, create rules, and develop digital literacy. By doing this, we may design a world in which technical improvements benefit society as a whole.

3.1 The Digital Revolution

The fast development and fusion of digital technologies, which have drastically changed several facets of human life, is referred to as the "Digital Revolution." It covers the broad uptake and use of computers, the internet, mobile devices, and other digital technologies that have transformed communication, information access, company operations, and personal lives. The development of electronic computers and the creation of the internet in the middle of the 20th century established the groundwork for the digital era, which is when the Digital Revolution began.

The exponential rise in processing power and the shrinking of electrical parts are two major forces behind the digital revolution. According to Moore's Law, which bears the name of Intel co-founder Gordon Moore, the number of transistors on a microchip doubles about every two years, increasing computing power. Smaller, quicker, and more powerful computers that can execute complicated tasks and store enormous quantities of data have been made possible because to the rapid development of technology.

The Digital Revolution has benefited greatly from the internet's ability to link gadgets and people throughout the world. The internet was first created for academic and military use, but it swiftly expanded into a worldwide network of linked computers that aided in the sharing of knowledge and the creation of new digital services. The World Wide Web's introduction in the early 1990s increased the adoption of digital technology by offering a simple interface for information access and exchange. By providing instant messaging, email, video conferencing, and social media platforms—platforms that transcend time and space—the internet has transformed communication.

The way companies run and engage with consumers has changed dramatically as a result of the Digital Revolution's substantial effects on a variety of sectors. E-commerce has become a powerful force, enabling both consumers and enterprises to do online business from the convenience of their homes. Traditional retail strategies have been upended by online marketplaces like Amazon and Alibaba, which has resulted in the demise of physical shops and the emergence of digital storefronts. With the advent of internet banking, mobile payments, and cryptocurrencies, the digitization of financial services has completely transformed the banking and payment business.

The Digital Revolution has democratized information exchange and access. Information is now more widely available and more reasonably priced because to the growth of digital material including news articles, movies, and music. People now have the ability to contribute to, exchange, and consume information and entertainment on a global scale thanks to online platforms like Wikipedia, YouTube, and Spotify. The emergence of social media has furthered this tendency by enabling individuals to organize for social and political issues, connect and cooperate across geographic borders, and share personal experiences.

The way we work and study has also changed as a result of the digital revolution. Cloud computing, video conferencing, and collaboration tools have made remote employment and digital nomadism more prevalent. Along with flexibility and work-life balance, this change has given people and companies new options in the economy. Through online learning platforms, which provide a worldwide audience access to courses and instructional materials, education has also undergone a change.

The Digital Revolution has not, however, been without difficulties and worries. As digital systems grow more linked, cybersecurity concerns including data breaches, identity theft, and cyberattacks have increased in frequency. As governments and businesses gather, store, and analyze people's personal data, privacy issues have also surfaced. Marginalized populations and developing nations face challenges to participation in the digital age due to the digital gap, which is defined by uneven access to digital technology.

The Digital Revolution doesn't seem to be slowing down in the near future. Artificial intelligence, blockchain, the Internet of Things (IoT), and virtual/augmented reality are some of the emerging technologies that have the potential to significantly change businesses and civilizations. These technologies have the power to boost decision-making, automate repetitive operations, increase healthcare results, and provide immersive digital experiences. They must be carefully studied because of the ethical, legal, and social considerations that their implementation also brings up.

The digital revolution has changed not just how we interact and do business, but also how we consume information and entertainment. The popularity of streaming services like Netflix, Hulu, and Spotify has upended established systems for distributing material. Users of these platforms have on-demand access to a huge collection of films, TV episodes, and musical selections, enabling individualized and immersive entertainment experiences. User-generated content has also emerged as a result of the digitization of media, with websites and apps like YouTube and TikTok making it possible for users to produce, distribute, and make money from their own original material.

The Digital Revolution has significantly improved healthcare and medicine in addition to entertainment. Patient care and access to healthcare services have increased thanks to the digitalization of medical data, the growth of telemedicine, and the usage of wearable technology. Healthcare providers may now contact patients in faraway locations and give them real-time medical advice thanks to remote monitoring and virtual consultations. Additionally, big data analytics and artificial intelligence have the potential to change personalized medicine, drug development, and diagnostics, resulting in more successful therapies and improved patient outcomes.

The Digital Revolution has an influence on both urban planning and transportation. A new idea known as "smart cities" envisions the integration of digital technology into urban infrastructure in order to improve efficiency, sustainability, and quality of life. The way we travel cities has changed because to intelligent transportation technologies like GPS navigation, traffic control systems, and ride-sharing platforms, which have decreased congestion and increased transportation efficiency. Smart homes, smart grids, and effective resource management are made possible by the Internet of Things (IoT), which enables the integration of numerous devices and systems.

The way we engage in democracy and political processes has also been transformed by the digital revolution. Platforms on social media have developed into effective instruments for political mobilization, enabling people to express their thoughts, establish movements, and hold governments responsible. Rapid information dissemination has both beneficial and bad effects, as the transmission of false information and fake news has grown to be a major problem. Discussions on rules and ethical issues in the digital sphere have been sparked by social media's impact on elections and political debate.

Addressing the difficulties and dangers associated with the current digital revolution is crucial as we see it unfold. Cybersecurity threats are always changing, necessitating strong protective measures for vital infrastructure and sensitive data. To protect individual privacy and stop abuse, data privacy laws and ethical guidelines must be created and implemented. For everyone, regardless of socioeconomic status, to have equal access to digital technology and opportunities, the digital gap must be closed.

3.2 Artificial Intelligence and Machine Learning

Machine learning (ML) and artificial intelligence (AI) have become two transformational technologies that are changing many sectors and how people live and work. The term artificial intelligence (AI) describes the creation of intelligent computers that can mimic human intellect and carry out activities that traditionally call for human cognition. Contrarily, ML is a branch of AI that focuses on making it possible for computers to learn from data and develop over time without explicit programming.

Numerous industries, including healthcare, banking, transportation, manufacturing, and entertainment, have benefited from the use of AI and ML. Medical picture analysis, illness diagnosis, and the creation of individualized treatment regimens are all done in the field of healthcare using AI and ML algorithms. AI-powered algorithms are used in finance for trading strategies, risk analysis, and fraud detection. In the field of transportation, self-driving vehicles mainly depend on ML algorithms to assess their surroundings and make instantaneous judgments.

Data is the main engine underlying AI and ML. These technologies depend on being able to gather, store, and analyse enormous volumes of data. Data fuels AI and ML systems, enabling them to discover trends, forecast the future, and provide insights. The proliferation of connected devices and the emergence of the Internet of Things (IoT) have increased the amount and diversity of data being produced, opening up several potential for AI and ML applications.

supervised learning, unsupervised learning, and reinforcement learning are three major categories for ML algorithms. Algorithms are trained on labeled data in supervised learning, when both the input and the result are known. This enables the algorithm to understand how the input and output are mapped, allowing it to generate predictions about data that has not yet been seen. The algorithm discovers patterns and structures in the data without explicit direction in unsupervised learning, which works with unlabeled data. Through reinforcement learning, an algorithm is taught to choose actions that will maximize a reward signal.

Deep learning, a method used often in machine learning (ML), is based on artificial neural networks. Due to its outstanding performance in tasks like voice recognition, picture recognition, and natural language processing, deep learning has become very popular in recent years. Deep neural networks are made up of many linked layers of nodes, or neurons, that resemble the architecture of the human brain. These networks learn to represent data in hierarchical ways, which enables them to extract intricate characteristics and patterns.

While AI and ML provide enormous potential, they also present difficulties and ethical dilemmas. Massive data collecting and utilization raises questions about data security and privacy. As AI algorithms have the potential to reinforce pre-existing social prejudices found in the data, there are also worries regarding bias and fairness in them. To guarantee the appropriate and ethical use of AI and ML technologies, it is essential to create ethical frameworks and rules.

There are ongoing research projects to push the limits of AI and ML as these technologies develop. In order to increase the effectiveness, interpretability, and resilience of AI and ML systems, researchers are investigating novel architectures, algorithms, and approaches. For instance, explainable AI tries to create models that can provide clear and understandable justifications for their judgments and forecasts. Another developing field is federated learning, which focuses on building ML models using distributed data sources without disclosing private data.

The influence of artificial intelligence (AI) and machine learning (ML) on commercial operations, healthcare, education, and even routine jobs has been significant. In its widest meaning, artificial intelligence (AI) is the emulation of human intellect in computational systems that can carry out operations that ordinarily demand for human cognition. ML, on the other hand, is a branch of AI that focuses on creating models and algorithms that let computers learn from data and become better with practice.

There are a number of variables that have fueled the rapid development of AI and ML technology. First and foremost, the exponential expansion of data has made it possible to construct and train AI and ML models using an abundance of data. Unprecedented amounts of data have been produced by the digital age from a variety of sources, including social media, sensors, and online platforms. Utilizing this data, computers are trained to spot trends, forecast future events, and deduce hidden information.

Additionally, the processing and analysis of enormous volumes of data have been made possible by improvements in computer power and the availability of scalable infrastructure. Model development for AI and ML has been sped up by to high-performance computers, cloud computing, and specialized hardware like graphics processing units (GPUs). With the help of these technical developments, it is now possible to solve complicated issues that were previously thought to be unsolvable.

There are several areas where AI and ML are having an influence. AI has the ability to transform personalized medicine, medication development, and diagnostics in the field of healthcare. X-rays and MRI pictures may be analyzed by ML algorithms to find anomalies and help clinicians make precise diagnosis. Electronic health information may be mined by AI-powered systems to find trends and forecast illness outcomes, allowing proactive and individualized therapy.

For fraud detection, algorithmic trading, risk assessment, and customer service in the financial industry. Large amounts of financial data may be analyzed by ML algorithms to spot abnormalities and spot fraudulent activity in real-time. The whole banking and financial experience is improved by AI-powered chatbots and virtual assistants, which provide individualized client assistance and suggestions.

The use of AI and ML has significantly improved the transportation sector as well. For instance, self-driving vehicles depend on complex ML algorithms to sense their surroundings, make snap judgments, and maneuver safely. To comprehend their surroundings and respond to changing road conditions, these autonomous cars make use of sensor data from cameras, lidar, and radar. Self-driving vehicles have the potential to lead to increased road safety, less traffic, and more mobility for those with impairments.

Another industry where AI and ML have the potential to revolutionize current teaching methods is education. Intelligent tutoring systems can adjust to the demands of certain pupils to provide individualized learning opportunities. Chatbots and virtual assistants may aid students with their studies and offer answers to their inquiries thanks to natural language processing technology. AI-powered systems may also examine student performance data to pinpoint areas that want development and provide customized advice.

While AI and ML have many benefits, there are also risks and ethical issues to be aware of. Due to the enormous quantity of data that AI systems gather and analyse, privacy issues are raised. Privacy protection and data security are of utmost importance. Bias in AI algorithms is a serious problem as well. Because ML models draw their learning from past data, they could reinforce the biases and prejudices that are already present in the data. It is important to work toward creating impartial AI systems that do not reinforce social injustices.

Collaborations across disciplines are essential to addressing these issues. For the development, application, and usage of AI and ML technologies, ethical frameworks and rules must be defined. To guarantee the ethical and accountable use of these potent technologies, cooperation between engineers, politicians, and ethicists is required.

There is a lot of promise for AI and ML in the future. The goal of ongoing research is to make AI systems more comprehensible and interpretable so that users can comprehend the decision-making process. To improve the capabilities of AI and ML models, researchers are investigating innovative topologies like transformers and generative adversarial networks (GANs). The developing topic of federated learning also focuses on training ML models on distributed data sources without sacrificing privacy.

A new age of technical development has arrived thanks to AI and ML, which have the potential to change many different sectors and businesses. Our world is changing as a result of AI systems' capacity to evaluate vast amounts of data, learn from it, and make wise judgments. However, it is crucial to address the moral issues and make sure that ML and AI technologies are created and used ethically. AI and ML will surely continue to affect our future with continuing research and innovation, creating new opportunities and enhancing human skills.

3.3 Automation and Robotics

Robotics and automation are becoming strong technologies that are changing many sectors and how people live and work. Robotics deals with the design, development, and usage of robots to automate processes and complete difficult jobs, while automation refers to the use of computer software, machines, or other systems to carry out activities without human involvement. These technologies have the ability to work together to increase production, increase efficiency, and open up new opportunities in a variety of industries.

Automation and robots have been very important in manufacturing for reducing production procedures and increasing productivity. Industrial robots are becoming a familiar sight in industries, executing labor-intensive, repetitive jobs quickly and precisely. These robots can do jobs that would otherwise need human laborers in dangerous or boring conditions, such as assembling, welding, painting, and packing. Automation and robotics integration in manufacturing has raised productivity, raised product quality, and decreased costs, enhancing organizations' competitiveness.

Automation and robots are being used in industries other than manufacturing, including healthcare, logistics, agriculture, and transportation. Robots may help with operations, carry out delicate treatments, and enhance patient care in the field of healthcare. The maintenance of medical data, appointment scheduling, and inventory control may all be done effectively thanks to automation technologies. Robots are used in logistics and warehousing to monitor inventory, pick orders, and transport packages, which improves the efficiency and speed of supply chain activities. Drones and autonomous vehicles are employed in agriculture for automated harvesting, crop monitoring, and precision farming, helping farmers to maximize yields and resource efficiency. Autonomous cars have the potential to revolutionize how we travel and move things, making it safer, more effective, and less reliant on human drivers.

The service sector has also been significantly impacted by automation and robots. Virtual assistants and chatbots are being used more often to answer consumer questions, provide tailored suggestions, and speed up customer care procedures. For data analysis, predictive modeling, and decision-making in fields like finance, marketing, and customer relationship management, automation technologies are employed. Employees may concentrate on more complicated and creative work by automating regular and repetitive operations, which encourages innovation and value creation.

Although automation and robots have many advantages, they also spark worries about the future of employment and job displacement. In industries that rely primarily on manual labor, there is a danger of job losses when robots take over certain jobs. It's crucial to remember, too, that robots and automation also provide up new work prospects. These technologies need trained people in disciplines like robotics engineering, software development, and data analysis for their creation, implementation, and maintenance. The advent of the gig economy and the necessity for professionals with knowledge of maintaining and optimizing automated systems are examples of how automation may also result in the formation of whole new businesses and professions.

Robotics and automation-related ethical issues also come into play. Questions about these technologies' capacity for making decisions, responsibility, and possible biases are raised as they grow more sophisticated and autonomous. The ethical design and programming of automation systems and robots is essential, taking into consideration the effects on people, society, and the environment.

Automation and robots are now essential to society's progress because they shape how we engage with technology and alter many areas of our everyday life. These technologies are altering the way we experience our homes and offer care for those in need, from the comfort of home automation systems that regulate lighting, heating, and security to the usage of robotic companions for the elderly or those with disabilities.

Automation and robotics are having a huge influence on education through fostering engaging learning environments. In order to engage pupils, encourage critical thinking, and improve problem-solving abilities, educational robots are used in classrooms. These machines may help instructors deliver courses, provide personalised teaching, and encourage students' creativity and ingenuity. The use of automation systems in school administration helps to streamline administrative processes including scheduling, record-keeping, and grading.

Exploration and scientific inquiry are two areas where automation and robots are used. Robotic rovers have been crucial to space research because they have allowed us to collect useful information and pictures from far-off planets and celestial bodies. These rovers can go through difficult terrain, gather samples, and carry out research in places that are hostile to people or inaccessible to them. Underwater robots also supports marine exploration and research by enabling researchers to map underwater environments, investigate marine ecosystems, and keep an eye on coral reef health.

With the incorporation of automation and robots, the healthcare sector is going through a radical change. With unmatched accuracy, surgical robots let surgeons carry out minimally invasive treatments, lowering the chance of complications and increasing patient outcomes. Healthcare operations including medicine administration, patient monitoring, and data analysis are becoming more efficient and precise thanks to automation solutions. Robotic prostheses and exoskeletons are improving people with physical impairments' mobility and quality of life, allowing them to reclaim their independence and engage more fully in society.

Automation and robots have significantly advanced the fields of logistics and transportation. Self-driving vehicles and trucks have the potential to make roadways safer, relieve traffic, and increase fuel economy. Delivery drones are being tried for fast and effective product delivery, especially in locations with difficult terrain or underdeveloped infrastructure. Additionally, autonomous robots are being used in warehouses and fulfillment centers to streamline the operations of inventory management, order fulfillment, and package sorting.

Even the creative arts and entertainment sectors are being impacted by automation and robots. Large volumes of data may be analyzed by AI-powered algorithms to provide individualized suggestions for music, movies, and other types of entertainment. The immersive and interactive experiences offered by virtual reality (VR) and augmented reality (AR) technologies are revolutionizing the way we consume media and telling stories. Additionally, automation techniques are being employed to enhance visual effects and streamline procedures in the creation of movies and animations.

It is essential to discuss the ethical issues and make sure that these technologies are developed and used responsibly as automation and robots progress. It is important to carefully address concerns about data privacy, security, and the potential for exploitation or abuse of automated systems and robots. To protect against possible hazards and assure openness, accountability, and justice, rules and regulations must be put in place.

Numerous sectors and facets of our life are being revolutionized by automation and robots, creating prospects for improved production, efficiency, and innovation. These technologies are having a significant impact on everything from industry and healthcare to education, exploration, and entertainment. As we embrace and negotiate this robots and automation era, it is crucial to find a balance between using the advantages they bring and solving the difficulties they pose, all the while respecting ethical standards and making sure that technological integration is human-centric. Automation and robots have the ability to improve our lives, spur innovation, and build a more inclusive and sustainable future with responsible development and implementation.

3.4 Biotechnology and Genetic Engineering

The sciences of biotechnology and genetic engineering, which are interrelated, have completely changed how we see and work with biological things. While genetic engineering mainly focuses on the change of an organism's genetic material, biotechnology comprises a broad range of methods and tools that harness biological systems for a variety of purposes.

DNA, the life's blueprint, is at the heart of biotechnology and genetic engineering. Scientists have unlocked the power to control genetic information, enabling them to change the traits of creatures, by researching the structure and function of DNA. Numerous sectors, including agriculture, health, environmental research, and industrial manufacture are greatly impacted by this.

Crop productivity has changed as a result of biotechnology in agriculture. Scientists may incorporate desired qualities into plants by genetic engineering, such as improved nutritional value and higher resistance to pests, diseases, and environmental challenges. Genetically modified plants have the potential to boost agricultural yields, enhance food output, and lessen the need for chemical fertilizers and pesticides. The long-term effects of this technology on ecosystems and public health, however, also spark ethical questions and discussions.

In medicine, genetic engineering and biotechnology have created new possibilities for illness detection, treatment, and prevention. Genetic testing enables early intervention and individualized care by identifying people who are at risk of developing certain genetic illnesses. Recombinant DNA technology has also enabled the creation of genetically altered creatures or cell lines that can produce therapeutic proteins like insulin, growth factors, and antibodies. These innovations have transformed the pharmaceutical sector and improved patient outcomes.

The study of the environment also heavily utilizes genetic engineering. Microorganisms may be genetically altered to clean up oil spills, decompose pollutants, or make biofuels from renewable resources. Additionally, genetically modified mosquitoes have been created to reduce the number of disease-carrying insects and fight vector-borne illnesses like malaria and dengue fever. These examples show how biotechnology may be used to alleviate environmental issues and encourage sustainable habits.

Biotechnology has also benefitted industrial manufacturing. Numerous industrial operations, including the creation of biofuels, detergents, and textiles, require enzymes generated by genetically altered microbes. By providing alternatives to conventional manufacturing processes, these bio-based goods lessen dependency on fossil fuels and have a less negative effect on the environment.

Despite the amazing accomplishments of biotechnology and genetic engineering, there are still concerns about morality and ethical issues. Concerns regarding unintended repercussions and ecological disruptions are raised by the possible dangers connected with genetically modified organisms (GMOs) and the discharge of genetically engineered organisms into the environment. Additionally, discussions about intellectual property rights and access to genetic resources have been spurred by the ownership and patenting of genetically modified seeds and organisms.

Many nations have put in place regulatory frameworks and rules to guarantee the proper and safe use of genetic engineering and biotechnology. These frameworks are designed to evaluate the advantages and disadvantages of genetically modified organisms, provide labeling guidelines for GM goods, and safeguard consumer and environmental rights.

The term "biotechnology" refers to a broad variety of methods and procedures that use living things like cells, organisms, or proteins to create new goods or enhance old ones. Ancient methods of producing food and drinks, including fermentation, have their origins in this discipline. The ability to influence and alter biological systems has, however, risen dramatically thanks to the development of scientific understanding and technical means.

A branch of science called genetic engineering specializes in precisely changing an organism's genetic makeup. This is accomplished by adding new genes into an organism's genome or altering already-existing genes there. Utilizing specialized tools like restriction enzymes to cut DNA at precise locations, DNA ligases to glue DNA fragments together, and vectors like plasmids to introduce genetic information into host organisms are all part of genetic engineering methods.

The creation of genetically modified organisms (GMOs) is one of the most important uses of genetic engineering. GMOs are living things whose genetic makeup has been changed to manifest certain traits or qualities. GMOs have been created specifically for the agricultural sector to have qualities like better nutritional value and higher resilience to pests, diseases, and herbicides. In order to reduce the use of chemical pesticides, genetically modified crops such as Bt cotton and Bt maize, for instance, release a toxin that is detrimental to certain pests.

The realm of medicine has benefited from genetic engineering as well. Scientists have made significant progress in understanding the genetic causes of illnesses via the modification of genes. Since gene therapies attempt to rectify genetic defects or introduce therapeutic genes into patients, this information has cleared the road for their development. CRISPR-Cas9 and other gene editing technologies have completely changed the field by giving scientists very accurate and effective tools for changing certain genes. This has created new opportunities for the treatment of cancer, genetic abnormalities, and other illnesses.

Genetic engineering has been useful in the creation of recombinant proteins in addition to medicinal uses. In this procedure, a gene encoding the desired protein is inserted into a host organism, such yeast or bacteria, which subsequently makes the protein in enormous amounts. Recombinant proteins have a wide range of applications, from enzymes employed in industrial processes like the manufacturing of medicines or the generation of biofuels to medicinal proteins like insulin and growth hormones.

Environmental research and conservation have advanced thanks to biotechnology and genetic engineering. By boosting the capacity of microorganisms to digest poisons and contaminants, researchers have created techniques to restore contaminated environments. This may aid in ecosystem restoration and the cleaning up of polluted places. By examining their genetic variety and creating conservation plans, genetic tools are also utilized to research and protect endangered species.

Although biotechnology and genetic engineering have many advantages, there are also issues that need to be resolved. When utilizing or introducing genetically modified goods into the environment, safety is a crucial factor to take into account. To guarantee the preservation of ecosystems, human health, and biodiversity, rigorous risk assessments and evaluation of possible dangers are essential. It is also necessary to take into account ethical issues, such as the possibility of unintended effects and the fair distribution of advantages.

Genetic engineering and biotechnology have altered several industries and have the capacity to address difficult problems. These disciplines have changed our knowledge of living things and our capacity to control them for human advantage, from agriculture to health, environmental science to industrial manufacture. To address the ethical, social, and environmental ramifications of new technologies, nevertheless, responsible research, regulation, and public discourse are crucial. We can harness the potential of biotechnology and genetic engineering to create a sustainable and affluent future by finding a balance between innovation and ethical usage.

3.5 Nanotechnology and Materials Science

Numerous sectors of science, engineering, and technology have been changed by the intersection of nanotechnology and materials science. Nanotechnology is the study and application of materials at the nanoscale, or distances between 1 and 100 nanometers. On the other side, materials science investigates the composition, structure, and behavior of materials. Unprecedented prospects for innovation and improvements in a variety of sectors are presented when these two disciplines come together.

New opportunities for creating and producing materials with improved characteristics and functions have been made possible by advances in nanotechnology. Scientists may produce structures and gadgets with special properties that are not seen in bulk materials by altering materials at the atomic and molecular level. In disciplines like electronics, health, energy, and environmental research, this capacity to manipulate materials at such a tiny scale has produced amazing discoveries.

Nanotechnology has been instrumental in the creation of more compact, quick, and effective electrical devices. For instance, the development of ever-more potent and energy-efficient microchips has changed the semiconductor industry with the advent of nanoscale transistors. Nanomaterials with remarkable electrical characteristics, including carbon nanotubes and graphene, are the best choice for developing the electronics of the future.

Nanotechnology has significantly improved medication delivery, diagnosis, and therapy in the medical profession. The exact distribution of medicinal medicines is made possible by the functionalization of nanoparticles to target certain cells or tissues, minimizing adverse effects. Nanomaterials have also showed promise in imaging methods, providing more precise and sensitive early illness diagnosis.

Another field where nanotechnology has had a significant impact is energy. Researchers have improved solar cells' performance and decreased their cost by incorporating nanomaterials into them, making solar energy a more practical and sustainable alternative. For the growth of electric cars and renewable energy systems, nanotechnology has also helped the creation of high-capacity batteries for energy storage and more effective catalysts for fuel cells.

Nanotechnology provides possible answers to urgent worldwide concerns in the field of environmental research. Nanomaterials, for instance, may be used in water purification procedures to more efficiently remove impurities and pollutants. Environmental factors may be accurately detected and monitored using nanosensors, which helps with resource management and pollution prevention. Additionally, nanotechnology-based methods have the potential to revolutionize waste management and make it possible to create more environmentally friendly and durable products.

The synthesis and characterisation of nanomaterials have significantly advanced as a result of the interaction between nanotechnology and materials science. By modifying materials' composition, size, form, and structure at the nanoscale, scientists may now create materials with specific qualities. Modern methods for controlling the synthesis of materials, such as molecular beam epitaxy, chemical vapor deposition, and self-assembly, provide materials that are more effective and useful.

Additionally, methods for nanoscale characterisation have become crucial for comprehending the atomic and molecular behavior of materials. Scientists can see and examine materials with amazing resolution using methods like transmission electron microscopy, atomic force microscopy, and X-ray diffraction, giving them insights into their structure, flaws, and characteristics. For improving material design and creating new applications, this information is essential.

Despite the many advantages of nanotechnology and materials science, there are also significant concerns about their safety and possible negative effects on the environment. If nanoparticles are discharged into the environment or come into contact with living things, their special qualities might be dangerous. Therefore, in order to guarantee the protection of both human health and the environment, responsible development and use of nanotechnology need thorough risk assessment and regulation.

Our perception of and interactions with the environment have changed as a result of nanotechnology and materials science. Scientists and engineers have developed the capacity to regulate the basic components of materials as a result of their exploration and manipulation of matter at the nanoscale. This has allowed them to create unique materials with amazing characteristics and capabilities.

The effect that nanotechnology has had on the electronics sector is one of the technology's amazing elements. Researchers are investigating nanoscale materials and gadgets as a result of the ongoing desire for smaller, quicker, and more potent electronic devices. Nanoelectronics was made possible by the downsizing of electronic parts like transistors made possible by nanotechnology. In comparison to their bigger counterparts, these nanoscale transistors function better, and they have cleared the way for the development of wearable electronics, flexible electronics, and even transparent and flexible electronics.

Nanotechnology has completely changed how medical professionals diagnose and treat patients, as well as how drugs are delivered. Nanoparticles may be functionalized to selectively target cancer cells or deliver medications to particular places inside the body because to their special size-dependent features. This focused strategy reduces the negative effects on healthy tissues while simultaneously improving the efficacy of therapies. Additionally, the use of nanomaterials in medical imaging methods has made it possible to diagnose illnesses like cancer and neurological problems more precisely and sensitively.

Nanotechnology has had a significant influence on energy as well. In terms of enhancing energy production, storage, and conservation, nanomaterials have demonstrated to be quite promising. For instance, solar energy is now a more practical and affordable alternative because to the use of nanomaterials in solar cells, which has enhanced their efficiency. High-capacity batteries have also been made possible by nanotechnology, enabling effective energy storage in portable electronics, electric cars, and renewable energy systems. Nanomaterials have also been used in energy-saving innovations like smart windows that dynamically regulate heat and light transmission, resulting in lower energy use in buildings.

Nanotechnology has the ability to solve some of the most critical problems confronting our world in the field of environmental research. Nanomaterials may be used in water treatment procedures to more efficiently remove impurities and pollutants. They can work as catalysts to efficiently and deliberately transform contaminants into less dangerous ones. Nanosensors provide very sensitive environmental parameter detection and monitoring, which aids in resource management and pollution prevention. Furthermore, by allowing the creation of sustainable materials with improved durability and recyclability, nanotechnology has the potential to completely transform waste management.

The synthesis and characterisation of materials have made significant strides thanks to the merging of nanotechnology and materials science. With today's technology, scientists are able to precisely manipulate the composition, structure, and characteristics of materials. Molecular self-assembly, nanolithography, and atomic layer deposition are a few of the techniques that may be used to create materials with complex structures and specialized functions. A greater knowledge of materials' behavior at the nanoscale is made possible by improved characterisation instruments like scanning probe microscopy and spectroscopic methods, which also enable further material design optimization.

Despite the enormous promise of nanotechnology and materials science, it is crucial to address the moral, medical, and security concerns related to its creation and use. It is critical to comprehend the possible effects of nanomaterials on environmental quality and human health as they are used in more and more consumer goods and industrial applications. To guarantee the safe and sustainable development of nanotechnology, rigorous risk assessment, laws, and ethical procedures are required.

In conclusion, the symbiotic relationship between nanotechnology and materials science has transformed a number of sectors and created new avenues for technological development. The capacity to alter materials at the nanoscale has produced amazing advances and game-changing applications in fields including electronics, health, energy, and environmental research. We may anticipate new discoveries that will impact the future and enhance our lives in a variety of ways as long as research and development in these sectors continue. For the sake of society and the environment, it is crucial to seize the potential offered by nanotechnology while guaranteeing its ethical and sustainable use.

Chapter 4

The Impact of Technology on Politics

4. Introduction

Technology has had a profound influence on politics, affecting political institutions and changing the dynamics of power. Recent technological developments have transformed government operations, information sharing, public involvement, and political campaigns. For politicians, voters, and governments, technology has brought both possibilities and difficulties, from the emergence of social media to the spread of big data analytics.

The way that technology has changed political campaigns is one key way that it has affected politics. Digital initiatives have complemented, and in some instances supplanted, conventional means of voter outreach including canvassing homes and television ads. Social media sites like Facebook, Twitter, and Instagram are increasingly widely used by campaigns to interact with voters, spread messages, and energize supporters. Campaigning is now more successful and economical because to the ability to target certain demographics and customize messaging. But this digital environment has also sparked worries about data privacy, fake news, and the impact of algorithms on voting behavior.

The way political information is distributed has also undergone a transformation thanks to technology. Information is now more readily available to the public because to the development of the internet and 24-hour news cycles. Bypassing conventional gatekeepers, citizens may now get news and political material from a variety of internet sources. The democratization of knowledge has given people more power and chances for political engagement. However, technology has also contributed to the dissemination of false information and the development of echo chambers, in which people are only exposed to material that supports their preexisting opinions. This has exacerbated divisiveness and made it difficult to come to consensus on political problems.

Technology has also been essential for civic activity and participation. Social media platforms have developed into effective tools for planning demonstrations, organizing neighborhoods, and promoting political agendas. Social media has been used by movements like the Arab Spring and Black Lives Matter to rally support, magnify their voices, and hold governments responsible. Technology has given underrepresented groups a forum to be heard and has upended conventional power systems. However, the digital gap raises issues since not everyone has access to technology and online platforms equally, which may worsen already-existing inequities.

Technology has affected how governments operate, in addition to campaigns and public participation.

Administrative procedures have been digitized via e-governance projects, which has increased their efficiency and transparency. Government processes have been expedited via computerized voting machines, online portals for citizen services, and data-driven policymaking. Large volumes of data may now be gathered and analyzed by governments to help them make decisions and enhance public services. Thoughts regarding data security, personal information, and possible biases in algorithmic decision-making are also raised by these developments.

Technology has an effect on politics that transcends national borders. The growth of international political concerns and challenges is a result of the interconnection made possible by technology. Threats to cybersecurity, cyberwarfare, and the international dissemination of misinformation are becoming top priorities for governments. To overcome these obstacles and set universal standards and guidelines for the use of technology in politics, international cooperation is essential.

Technology has had a profound influence on politics, affecting political institutions and changing the dynamics of power. Recent technological developments have transformed government operations, information sharing, public involvement, and political campaigns. For politicians, voters, and governments, technology has brought both possibilities and difficulties, from the emergence of social media to the spread of big data analytics.

The way that technology has changed political campaigns is one key way that it has affected politics. Digital initiatives have complemented, and in some instances supplanted, conventional means of voter outreach including canvassing homes and television ads. Social media sites like Facebook, Twitter, and Instagram are increasingly widely used by campaigns to interact with voters, spread messages, and energize supporters. Campaigning is now more successful and economical because to the ability to target certain demographics and customize messaging. Candidates may now reach a wider audience than ever before because to the widespread distribution of political ads and propaganda. But this digital environment has also sparked worries about data privacy, fake news, and the impact of algorithms on voting behavior. Election integrity and the democratic process are at risk due to the widespread exploitation of personal data and the dissemination of misleading information.

The way political information is distributed has also undergone a transformation thanks to technology. Information is now more readily available to the public because to the development of the internet and 24-hour news cycles. The conventional gatekeepers, including newspapers and television networks, are no longer necessary for citizens to access news and political material. The democratization of knowledge has given people more power and chances for political engagement. Citizens who were previously underrepresented or disenfranchised now have a voice thanks to social media platforms, blogs, and independent news sources. Now, people may share their experiences, participate in political debates, and voice their ideas to the general public. However, technology has also contributed to the dissemination of false information and the development of echo chambers, in which people are only exposed to material that supports their preexisting opinions. This has exacerbated divisiveness and made it difficult to come to consensus on political problems. The pursuit of truth and the need of media literacy have emerged as essential components of contemporary political debate.

Technology has affected how governments operate, in addition to campaigns and public participation. Administrative procedures have been digitized via e-governance projects, which has increased their efficiency and transparency. Government processes have been expedited via computerized voting machines, online portals for citizen services, and data-driven policymaking. Large volumes of data may now be gathered and analyzed by governments to help them make decisions and enhance public services. Predictive analytics, for instance, may support the identification of areas that need intervention, optimize resource allocation, and improve the efficacy of governmental initiatives. Through online platforms and mobile apps, people may now submit comments, report problems, and take part in decision-making processes, which has increased citizen-government contact. Thoughts regarding data security, personal information, and possible biases in algorithmic decision-making are also raised by these developments. To maintain openness, accountability, and public confidence, technology must be used in governance in a responsible and ethical manner.

Technology has an effect on politics that transcends national borders. The growth of international political concerns and challenges is a result of the interconnection made possible by technology. Threats to cybersecurity, cyberwarfare, and the international dissemination of misinformation are becoming top priorities for governments. Governments must devise plans to safeguard their electronic systems and fend off cyberthreats. To overcome these obstacles and set universal standards and guidelines for the use of technology in politics, international cooperation is essential. In order to foster stability, security, and the moral use of technology in political settings, actions like international treaties, cooperative intelligence-sharing agreements, and coordinated cybersecurity activities are crucial.

4.1 Disrupting Traditional Power Structures

Long-standing traditional power structures have shaped and controlled how opportunities, resources, and power are distributed in society. However, a significant movement that aims to overthrow and oppose these entrenched structures has evolved in recent years. In recognition of the fact that conventional power systems often promote inequality, marginalization, and injustice, this movement is motivated by a desire for more inclusive and equitable society.

The realization that power is not dispersed fairly in society lies at the heart of the disruption of old power systems. Politics, the economy, and cultural influence have traditionally been dominated by a small number of people. For oppressed groups including women, people of color, LGBTQ+ persons, and those from lower socioeconomic backgrounds, this power imbalance has led to systematic disadvantages. By spreading power and giving previously underrepresented voices a chance to be heard, conventional power systems that are being disrupted seek to eliminate these inequalities.

Politics is one area where established power structures are being challenged. In the past, a small number of people have held the majority of the political power, often thanks to structures that benefit the well-off and connected. In contrast, underprivileged populations may now organize and mobilize in previously unthinkable ways thanks to grassroots movements and the growth of social media. As a result, a broad group of political leaders that push for progressive policies, speak for historically neglected populations, and question the existing quo have emerged. These movements aspire to build more representative and inclusive governments that put the needs and interests of all people first by upending conventional political power structures.

Challenges to the concentration of wealth and resources in the hands of a small number of affluent people and businesses are an economic component of upending established power systems. In many nations, income disparity has reached shockingly high levels, with the wealthy becoming wealthier while the underprivileged struggle to provide for their fundamental requirements. Due to this, there are now few prospects for upward mobility and a cycle of poverty. Economic justice movements call for equitable pay, workers' rights, and wealth redistribution in an effort to break this cycle. They advocate for economic systems that put the welfare of all people above the pursuit of profit for a select few and contest the exploitative business practices of big business.

Culture and media are another sector where conventional power systems are being challenged. Traditional media institutions have historically served as information gatekeepers, influencing social narratives and forming public opinion. The creation and sharing of knowledge has, however, become more democratic with the emergence of social media and digital platforms. People and groups that were formerly excluded or underrepresented may now express their experiences, question established myths, and call for representation in the media and popular culture. It is crucial for developing a more inclusive and varied society, where all viewpoints and experiences are welcomed and celebrated, that conventional power structures in media and culture be disrupted.

Dismantling established power structures also entails eliminating prejudice and oppression based on race, gender, sexual orientation, and other identification traits. Power systems are interrelated, and people may experience numerous types of oppression at once, according to intersectional movements. These movements fight for the rights and dignity of all people and oppose the supremacy of white, cisgender, heterosexual, and physically fit people. In order to advance social justice and equality, they seek to establish environments and frameworks that honor and elevate the perspectives and experiences of oppressed populations.

Reevaluating education institutions is necessary to undermine established power structures. Education has always been associated with social achievement and the ability to move ahead in society. However, through promoting certain information, pedagogical approaches, and cultural values, conventional educational institutions have often contributed to the persistence of inequality. Disrupting these systems entails identifying and resolving biases in the curriculum, encouraging inclusive teaching methods, and ensuring that everyone has equitable access to high-quality education, regardless of their socioeconomic status or identity. This involves promoting educational changes that give priority to social justice, cultural diversity, and critical thinking. We can enable people from disadvantaged populations to question cultural norms, follow their interests, and actively contribute to their communities by questioning conventional power systems inside education.

Sustainability initiatives and environmental activism are both examples of ways to challenge established power systems. As a result of traditional power systems' frequent preference for corporate profits and economic expansion above environmental issues, vulnerable populations have been displaced and the environment has deteriorated. By promoting eco-justice, renewable energy, and sustainable behaviors, environmental activists and grassroots groups are upending these hierarchies. They are opposing the influence of the fossil fuel industry, promoting laws and policies that safeguard the environment, and elevating the concerns of the communities who are disproportionately impacted by environmental devastation. These movements aim for a more sustainable and fair future for everyone by upending conventional power structures in the context of environmental activism.

Traditional power structures are being significantly disrupted by technology and digital platforms. People now have a platform to communicate, organize, and challenge traditional power dynamics thanks to the internet and social media. Marginalized populations may now raise awareness, share their stories, and hold those in authority responsible thanks to online activism and digital campaigns. Additionally, technology has increased information access, enabling people to educate themselves and challenge prevailing narratives. To stop future marginalization, it is crucial to overcome the digital gap and provide fair access to technology. Disrupting old power structures in the digital sphere requires aggressively combatting disinformation and online abuse while promoting online places that are welcoming, secure, and respectful of many viewpoints.

It is crucial to recognise that overturning established power systems is not without difficulties and opposition. Those who stand to gain from existing power structures often oppose change, utilizing their resources and influence to preserve the status quo. It takes persistent campaigning, community organization, coalition building, and legislative changes to remove these obstacles. It also calls for encouraging empathy, communication, and understanding among various cultures and socioeconomic groupings.

Traditional power structures are being disrupted in a complex and continuing process that affects many facets of society. It entails confronting and changing the social, political, economic, cultural, educational, environmental, and technical structures that support marginalization, discrimination, and inequality. This movement seeks to make the world more fair, egalitarian, and sustainable for all people by dispersing power, highlighting minority voices, encouraging inclusion, and calling for structural change. It calls for teamwork, endurance, and a dedication to overthrowing deeply ingrained structures of privilege and power.

4.2 Citizen Engagement and Participation

Participation and involvement of citizens are essential components of a democratic society's operation. It speaks to the active participation of residents in the development of their communities, the formation of policies, and decision-making processes. Governments may create a more inclusive and responsive governance system that represents the needs and ambitions of its population by encouraging people to become involved in public affairs.

The accessibility of information is important for public involvement and participation. To promote an educated populace, open and transparent avenues of communication between the government and its citizens are essential. This entails offering chances for public comment and input as well as easily available information regarding policies, programs, and activities of the government. Citizens can make better judgments and actively participate in public dialogue with greater information availability.

Town hall meetings and public discussions are frequent techniques used to promote citizen involvement. Through these forums, residents may communicate their ideas, worries, and proposals to decision-makers in the government. It gives people the chance to share their knowledge, engage in the formulation of policies that have an impact on their lives, and contribute to the decision-making process. Additionally, social media and internet platforms have considerably increased the potential for public involvement by providing greater participation and audience reach.

Engagement and involvement of citizens can entail cooperation and co-creation in addition to information and consultation. Citizens may be actively involved in the development, delivery, and assessment of public policies and services by their governments. Communities may co-create solutions that meet their particular needs and issues by soliciting feedback from a variety of stakeholders, including disadvantaged groups. This cooperative approach not only builds the social fabric and fosters a feeling of ownership among residents, but also improves the efficacy and legitimacy of governmental initiatives.

Participation and involvement of citizens may lead to a number of advantageous consequences for both individuals and society at large. Citizens are more likely to have a feeling of ownership and belonging in their communities when they are actively involved. Higher levels of social cohesiveness and enhanced faith in governmental institutions follow from this. Additionally, engaged people are more inclined to engage in volunteer work, community groups, and other civic projects, which benefits society's general resilience and well-being.

Participation and involvement of citizens also encourage creativity and innovation. Governments may take use of a wide variety of viewpoints, ideas, and skills by drawing on the collective intelligence of individuals. This may result in improved policy results, more successful problem-solving, and the identification of novel solutions to difficult problems. Engaged citizens may play a role in co-creation and problem-solving, assisting in the discovery of new problems, weaknesses in service provision, and opportunities for development.

Participation and involvement of citizens are also essential tools for keeping governments responsible. Citizens may monitor and examine governmental activities, programs, and expenditures by actively engaging in public affairs. This active engagement ensures that governments remain open, receptive, and responsible to the people they serve, acting as a check on possible power abuses and corruption. Thus, public participation enhances the overall integrity and effectiveness of democratic administration.

But despite all of its advantages, public involvement and participation confront a number of difficulties. The presence of structural obstacles that hinder some groups from fully participating is one significant impediment. Socioeconomic gaps, restricted access to technology and information, language hurdles, and prejudice towards people because of their gender, race, or disability are all examples of this. Governments and organizations must work proactively to guarantee inclusion and provide chances for participation for all individuals in order to solve these issues.

The indifference and disengagement of certain people with regard to public affairs is another problem. Citizens' involvement may be hampered by things like political cynicism, a lack of faith in the government, and the belief that their opinions won't be heard. In order to advance civic education and knowledge, inculcate a feeling of civic duty, and provide platforms that foster meaningful engagement, governments and civil society groups must collaborate.

As they encourage active citizenship, inclusion, openness, and accountability, citizen engagement and participation are crucial for the operation of democratic societies. Governments may guarantee that policies and initiatives are responsive to the needs and ambitions of the people they serve by incorporating individuals in decision-making processes.

The development of a better educated and aware populace is a major advantage of citizen involvement. People can make better judgments and effectively participate in public dialogue when they have access to pertinent information regarding government policies, programs, and projects. Governments must emphasize open and transparent communication channels in order to do this, making sure that information is available, simple to grasp, and widely shared.

The facilitation of citizen interaction is greatly aided through public consultations and town hall sessions. Citizens have the chance to communicate their ideas, worries, and proposals to legislators via these channels. It makes it possible for direct communication and engagement, which encourages a feeling of cooperation between the government and its citizens. A larger audience may now be reached and more involvement is possible thanks to social media and internet platforms, which have also increased the opportunities for citizen engagement.

Additionally, citizen participation extends beyond straightforward consultation and information exchange. Citizens actively engage in the development, delivery, and assessment of public policies and services via cooperation and co-creation. This strategy acknowledges the significant knowledge and experience that people may provide in helping to create more inclusive and successful policies. Governments may make sure that policies are adapted to suit the unique demands and difficulties encountered by various communities by incorporating a variety of stakeholders, including disadvantaged groups.

Participation and involvement of citizens can have significant societal advantages. Citizens are more likely to have a strong feeling of belonging and civic pride when they are actively involved in their communities and feel a sense of ownership. In turn, this promotes social cohesiveness, lessens social divides, and improves society's fabric as a whole. A more dynamic and resilient society results from engaged individuals who are also more inclined to take part in volunteer work, community groups, and other civic efforts.

Additionally, public participation fosters creativity and innovation. Governments are able to generate fresh insights, spot difficulties as they emerge, and come up with creative answers to difficult problems by drawing on the collective wisdom and varied viewpoints of the populace. This teamwork-based strategy promotes unconventional thinking, strengthens problem-solving skills, and produces better policy results.

Participation and involvement of citizens are essential for keeping governments responsible. Citizens who are actively interested in public affairs serve as watchdogs, keeping an eye on government spending, policies, and activities. This engagement actively prevents possible power abuses, corruption, and poor management. The integrity and effectiveness of democratic governance are improved because it makes sure that governments continue to be open, receptive, and responsible to the people they serve.

Nevertheless, despite the many advantages, there are issues with public involvement and participation that need to be resolved. The existence of structural obstacles that restrict the involvement of certain groups is one major obstacle. Full and equitable participation may be hindered by socioeconomic gaps, restricted access to information and technology, language hurdles, and discrimination based on gender, race, or disability. Governments and organizations must work proactively to guarantee inclusion, remove these obstacles, and provide chances for participation for all residents.

The indifference and disengagement of certain people with regard to public affairs is another problem. Citizens' involvement may be hampered by things like political cynicism, a lack of faith in the government, and the belief that their opinions won't be heard. Governments and civil society groups must make investments in civic education and awareness initiatives, inspire a feeling of civic duty, and provide platforms that foster meaningful involvement in order to solve this difficulty.

4.3 Surveillance and Privacy Concerns

As technology develops, privacy and surveillance issues have taken center stage in contemporary culture. The privacy of people is now more at danger than ever due to the widespread use of digital devices like smartphones and smart home systems as well as the gathering and analysis of enormous quantities of data. A contentious discussion about how to strike a balance between security and privacy has been prompted by the rapid development of surveillance technology by both public and commercial organizations.

Government monitoring is one of the main causes for worry. Governments all around the globe have developed a variety of monitoring systems in the name of national security and crime prevention. Individual privacy rights have come under attention because of mass monitoring programs like the contentious PRISM in the United States. Massive volumes of data, including conversations, internet activity, and even location data, have led some to wonder how far the government has gotten into people's private lives. Such monitoring techniques, according to critics, weaken civil rights and limit the freedom of speech and expression.

Private organizations have a crucial role in the surveillance and privacy issues. In the digital era, businesses gather and examine enormous volumes of personal data in order to customize their goods and services, target advertisements, and come to informed business judgments. A few examples of companies that collect and analyze a lot of user data are social networking platforms, search engines, and online shops. Although many people voluntarily provide their information to these services in return for the comfort and customization they provide, the possibility of misuse or abuse of this data raises serious concerns. Data breaches, illegal access to personal data, and the sale of user data have brought to light the dangers posed by the substantial digital traces we leave behind.

New monitoring techniques that were once the stuff of science fiction have also emerged as a result of technological breakthroughs. For instance, facial recognition technology is rapidly being used in police enforcement, airport security, and even social networking platforms. The possibility for misuse and privacy violations has been discussed in relation to the capacity to identify and monitor people based on their facial traits. The use of facial recognition technologies, according to critics, may result in mistaken identifications, widespread monitoring, and the deterioration of anonymity in public places since they are often implemented without the required control and restrictions.

Internet of Things (IoT) gadget proliferation has increased privacy issues. In addition to providing convenience and automation, linked products, wearable technology, and smart homes produce an unprecedented quantity of personal data. These gadgets capture every aspect of our life, from tracking our sleep patterns to documenting our everyday activities. IoT device connectivity raises questions about data security and the possibility of illegal access to private data. Even more privacy issues are presented by the idea of a "smart city," where different municipal systems are connected and monitored. Questions regarding how to strike the right balance between security, effectiveness, and personal privacy are raised by the ongoing collecting and analysis of data from sensors, surveillance cameras, and public records.

Addressing the related privacy issues is crucial as surveillance technologies develop further. Strong legal frameworks, efficient supervision, and open rules are needed to strike a compromise between security and privacy. Governments must implement laws that safeguard national security and individual privacy rights. To avoid exploitation and misuse of personal information, it is essential to have clear policies about data collecting, storage, and sharing. Similar to how public firms must follow moral guidelines when processing customer data, including clear permission processes and robust data security safeguards. Additionally, user education and awareness are vital because they enable people to make educated choices about their privacy and promote responsible technology usage.

The convergence of big data and machine learning algorithms is one factor that accentuates privacy and surveillance issues. The development of artificial intelligence (AI) and data analytics has made it feasible to glean insightful information from enormous volumes of gathered data. Although this has the potential to advance a number of social issues, including urban planning, transportation, and healthcare, it also presents questions over individual privacy. It is possible to manipulate people's preferences, beliefs, and choices when human behavior can be analyzed and predicted based on data patterns. Discussions on the moral ramifications and potential for discrimination and exploitation have been sparked by the use of tailored advertising, targeted political campaigns, and algorithmic decision-making systems.

Furthermore, privacy protection is challenged by the internet's and digital communication's worldwide reach.

Data moves freely across borders in today's linked globe, making it challenging to implement uniform privacy laws. There are differences in privacy rules across different nations due to their different approaches to data protection and monitoring techniques. This poses issues for anyone whose data may be monitored or kept in locations with laxer privacy rules. Debattions concerning privacy as a basic human right that ought to be protected regardless of nationality have also strained international ties and been sparked by disclosures of government monitoring operations that target foreign citizens.

Concerns about privacy and surveillance also apply to the healthcare industry. Healthcare delivery and patient monitoring have improved as a result of the digitalization of medical information, the usage of wearable health devices, and the use of telemedicine services. However, the delicate nature of health information presents serious privacy concerns. Medical record breaches may make private information regarding a person's medical history, genetics, and mental health history available. Unauthorized access to or distribution of such data may have serious repercussions, such as stigmatization, discrimination, and a decline in public confidence in the healthcare system. It's critical to strike a balance between the advantages of digital healthcare and strong data security safeguards in order to protect people's privacy and preserve public confidence.

Blockchain and other cutting-edge technology may provide answers to privacy issues. Blockchain technology allows for safe, decentralized data storage and transactions, giving users more control over their personal data. Blockchain can guarantee data openness and integrity by using cryptographic methods, while also enabling people to regulate their permission and share their data in only certain circumstances. However, there are still technological, governmental, and scalability obstacles to the broad acceptance and deployment of blockchain solutions.

A multifaceted strategy is required to reduce worries about monitoring and privacy. International organizations, governments, and legislators should work together to create comprehensive privacy rules and regulations that keep up with technology development. In order to ensure that privacy is taken into account from the outset of projects, privacy by design principles should be included into the creation of surveillance technologies and data-driven systems. Independent monitoring organizations and audits may ensure that surveillance techniques are transparent and accountable, and that they are carried out within the bounds of the law and with the necessary reasons. People may be empowered by education and public awareness campaigns to understand their privacy rights, make thoughtful decisions, and embrace privacy-enhancing technology and behaviors.

The fast development of technology, the extensive collecting and analysis of data, and the possibility for the exploitation or abuse of personal information give rise to privacy and surveillance issues. It is difficult to strike a balance between the advantages of monitoring for society growth and security and the defense of individual privacy rights. To guarantee privacy is protected in the digital era, there must be strong legislative frameworks, ethical standards, responsible actions by both public and private institutions, and active engagement from people. We may work toward a future where technology advancement and individual privacy live peacefully by proactively addressing these issues.

4.4 Cybersecurity and Digital Warfare

In our increasingly linked society, where technology and digital systems play a crucial part in our everyday lives, cybersecurity and digital warfare are crucial issues. The danger environment has changed as a result of the fast improvements in information technology, posing fresh difficulties for governments, businesses, and people to overcome. The term "cybersecurity" refers to the policies and procedures used to guard against unwanted access, interruption, and damage to computer systems, networks, and data. The use of technology and cyberspace as a battlefield, on the other hand, is referred to as "digital warfare" and is done in order to gain an edge over, interfere with, or destroy an enemy's digital infrastructure.

Cyber threats are more sophisticated and widespread than ever in the modern digital era, with possible repercussions ranging from financial losses to concerns to national security. In order to initiate cyberattacks, malicious actors, including hackers, cybercriminals, and state-sponsored organizations, take advantage of weaknesses in software, hardware, and user behavior. Malware infections, ransomware assaults, phishing scams, distributed denial-of-service (DDoS) attacks, and advanced persistent threats (APTs) are just a few of the many ways that these attacks might manifest. Such assaults may be carried out for a variety of reasons, including espionage, political objectives, or monetary gain.

Cybersecurity experts use a multi-layered strategy that combines preventative, investigative, and remedial actions to address these threats. Implementing security controls and best practices including firewalls, intrusion detection systems, encryption, powerful authentication methods, and security awareness training for users are examples of preventive measures. With the use of security monitoring tools, intrusion detection systems, and threat information, detective measures are primarily focused on quickly discovering and reacting to security issues. Following a successful cyber assault, corrective actions comprise repair and recovery activities such system restoration, vulnerability patches, and post-incident analysis to strengthen defenses.

Nations are rapidly realizing the significance of cyberspace as a strategic area in the context of digital warfare. Cyber operations may be used to outwit rivals, destroy their infrastructure, acquire information, or carry out clandestine activities. These operations might target vital infrastructure, governmental or military networks, or other countries' information systems. Due to the complexity of identification and responsibility and the many attempts made by attackers to mask their identities or use proxy servers, digital warfare has special obstacles.

Governments all around the globe have set up specialized cyber defense units and organizations tasked with safeguarding national interests online. These organizations seek to provide the tools necessary to successfully identify, stop, and react to cyberthreats. Since attacks may originate from anywhere in the globe and are not limited by physical borders, international collaboration and information exchange between governments have also become essential in addressing cyber threats. The Tallinn Manual on the International Law Applicable to Cyber Warfare and the Budapest Convention on Cybercrime both give rules for international cooperation on cybersecurity and set standards of conduct in cyberspace.

The landscape of cybersecurity is further complicated by the fast development of innovative technologies. The introduction of new attack surfaces and potential vulnerabilities is made possible by the Internet of Things (IoT), artificial intelligence (AI), cloud computing, and 5G networks. Keeping systems and devices secure becomes increasingly important as more of them are linked. A single compromised institution may have far-reaching effects across several businesses or sectors, therefore the increased complexity of supply chains and the dependence on third-party providers offer new dangers.

A multidisciplinary strategy is necessary to address the changing issues in cybersecurity and digital warfare. Along with technological fixes, it calls for the creation of legislative frameworks, public-private collaborations, and a culture of cybersecurity awareness. People and businesses need to take a proactive approach to cybersecurity by upgrading their software often, using secure passwords, and being wary of social engineering techniques. In order to provide professionals the knowledge and abilities they need to successfully protect against cyber threats, education and training programs must be in place.

Cybersecurity and digital warfare have become essential aspects of our everyday lives in the linked world of today. Our reliance on digital systems and networks has increased enormously as technology continues to evolve at a fast rate. As a result, the danger landscape has become more intricate, posing new difficulties for governments, organizations, and people to overcome.

Cybersecurity is the cornerstone for guarding against illegal access, interruption, and damage to networks, computer systems, and sensitive data. It includes a broad variety of techniques and policies intended to protect digital infrastructure. It is crucial to establish effective cybersecurity policies because cyber threats, such as those from hackers, cybercriminals, and state-sponsored organizations, are becoming more sophisticated.

On the other side, digital warfare centers on the use of technology and cyberspace as a battlefield. Utilizing digital resources to outwit, cripple, or gain an edge over an adversary's infrastructure. Nations understand that cyberspace is a key arena for digital warfare, where operations may target military networks, vital infrastructure, government systems, and other countries' information systems.

The reasons for cyberattacks might differ greatly. Some perpetrators want to make money, such as via ransomware attacks that demand payment from people or businesses. Others can be motivated by political ambitions with the intention of upsetting government functions or influencing public opinion. To obtain sensitive information or to carry out covert operations against other countries, state-sponsored organizations may engage in cyberespionage. The variety of cyber dangers and the significance of effective cybersecurity measures are highlighted by these reasons.

Security experts use a multi-layered strategy to combat these attacks. Implementing security controls and industry standards like as firewalls, intrusion detection systems, encryption, and robust authentication processes are examples of preventive measures. Additionally, it is essential for avoiding successful cyber assaults to educate consumers on security knowledge and safe online habits.

The goal of detective measures is to quickly discover and address security problems. Cybersecurity teams can identify and evaluate possible threats thanks to security monitoring technologies, intrusion detection systems, and threat intelligence. Early discovery enables prompt action, which lessens the effect of cyberattacks and stops more harm.

Remediating the impacts of a cyber assault and restoring compromised systems are considered corrective actions. To increase defenses and stop future assaults, this often entails recovering compromised systems, fixing vulnerabilities, and doing post-incident analysis.

The necessity for specialized cybersecurity units and organizations tasked with safeguarding national interests in cyberspace has been acknowledged by governments all over the globe. These organizations provide the tools necessary to successfully identify, stop, and react to cyberthreats. As assaults may come from anywhere in the globe, international collaboration and information exchange between governments are essential in the fight against cyber threats.

The Tallinn Manual on the International Law Applicable to Cyber Warfare and the Budapest Convention on Cybercrime both give rules for international cooperation on cybersecurity and set standards of conduct in cyberspace. These frameworks are designed to increase trust, encourage moral behavior, and stop bad actors.

The ongoing development of technology creates fresh difficulties for cybersecurity. There are more attack surfaces and possible vulnerabilities due to the growth of the Internet of Things (IoT) and the incorporation of artificial intelligence (AI) into different systems. Additionally adding to the complexity of cybersecurity plans are cloud computing and the rollout of 5G networks.

Additionally, the dependence on third-party suppliers and the interconnection of global supply networks increase risks. A single compromised corporation may have significant effects on several businesses or industries. By adopting strong supply chain security measures and carefully screening their providers, businesses must identify and reduce these risks.

A multidisciplinary strategy is necessary to address the changing issues in cybersecurity and digital warfare. Along with technological fixes, it calls for the creation of legislative frameworks, public-private collaborations, and a culture of cybersecurity awareness.

Organizations and individuals must take a proactive approach to cybersecurity. Software updates often, the use of secure passwords, and vigilance against social engineering techniques are best practices that everyone should follow. In order to provide professionals the knowledge and abilities they need to successfully protect against cyber threats, education and training programs must be in place.

Our increasingly digitalized society is characterized by the interdependence of cybersecurity and digital warfare. Prioritizing cybersecurity measures and creating strong defensive plans are essential given the pervasiveness of cyber threats and the potential harm they may do to people, businesses, and whole countries. We can jointly reduce the dangers presented by bad actors and guarantee the stability and security of our digital ecosystem by investing in cybersecurity technology, encouraging international cooperation, and increasing cybersecurity awareness.

4.5 Election Campaigns and Social Media

The way politicians interact with citizens and sway public opinion has been revolutionized by the intimate relationship between election campaigns and social media. Political candidates may now more than ever before access a larger audience, interact with supporters, and spread their campaign messages via social media platforms like Facebook, Twitter, Instagram, and YouTube.

The potential of social media to promote direct and quick connection between politicians and citizens is one of the major benefits it has during election campaigns. The creation of official social media profiles by candidates allows them to engage with voters, discuss their policy ideas, answer inquiries, and address issues. Voters may witness the candidates' in-the-moment comments and participation, which helps to humanize politicians and foster a feeling of authenticity.

Additionally, social media platforms provide political campaigns the perfect setting to target certain populations and modify their messaging appropriately. Campaigns may identify important voter categories and offer targeted material that speaks to their interests and concerns using data analytics and user profiling. By making sure their communications are delivered to the appropriate people, this focused strategy enables candidates to optimize the effect of their campaign messaging.

The pace and scope of information transmission during political campaigns have both been changed by social media. Social media platforms do not have the same time or space constraints as traditional media channels. Political candidates may instantaneously publish videos, articles, and live updates on their campaign, giving them the power to steer the conversation and act quickly when necessary. Rapid information exchange enables candidates to successfully sway public opinion and refute false narratives.

Additionally, campaigns may develop specific groups, pages, and hashtags that enable supporters to communicate with one another, debate campaign concerns, and plan events on social media, which has been very effective in motivating and organizing supporters. This feeling of belonging and common purpose energises supporters, prompting them to contribute money and time as well as actively engage in the campaign. Organizing offline activities like rallies, fundraisers, and door-to-door campaigns on social media also makes them more effective.

However, there are hazards and difficulties associated with the marriage of electoral campaigns with social media. The proliferation of false information and fake news is one of the main issues. Social media's viral nature may cause inaccurate or misleading information to spread quickly, which might have a big impact on the election process. With social media platforms introducing fact-checking processes and collaborating with other groups to confirm the veracity of material posted during campaigns, efforts to prevent disinformation have become vital.

Another issue is the possibility for echo chambers on social media, when users are only exposed to information that supports their own opinions and ideals. A good democratic dialogue requires a range of opinions, which might be hampered by this and reinforce preexisting prejudices. Furthermore, using social media as a main source of political information might create a fragmented public space where people only consume material that supports their beliefs, restricting their exposure to other viewpoints.

Social media may also make emotions and sensationalism more prominent in political campaigns. On social media platforms, messages that elicit strong emotional reactions often get greater attention and interaction, sometimes overshadowing serious policy discussions. To get the attention of social media users, candidates may feel pressured to employ provocative or controversial rhetoric, thus diverting attention from important problems and degrading the standard of political discourse.

The voting process has become more democratic thanks to social media since it gives underrepresented voices and grassroots movements a forum. In the past, conventional media outlets predominated the political conversation, making it difficult for newcomers or individuals with low means to become visible. Social media, on the other hand, enables political outsiders and activists to get in front of the public without the conventional gatekeepers. This has sparked the growth of social media-based movements, where people and organizations can unite, bring attention to pressing problems, and upend the existing quo.

Additionally, social media has made political campaigns more transparent and accountable. Social media platforms often record and publish the remarks and acts of candidates, making it simpler for voters and the media to hold them responsible for their words and deeds. This heightened scrutiny may aid in disclosing contradictions, preventing disinformation, and ensuring that candidates continue to respond to public concerns.

Social media also helped user-generated content and grassroots campaigning campaigns to take off. Volunteers and supporters may produce and distribute their own ads, films, and endorsements, essentially acting as spokespersons for the politicians they support. Social media's participatory nature enables campaigns to benefit from the ingenuity and zeal of its supporters, so broadening their appeal and influence.

On the other hand, worries regarding data security and privacy have increased as a result of social media's impact on elections. The massive quantities of personal information that social media platforms gather may be used for micro-targeting and customized messages, which raises concerns about the morality of doing so. To guarantee that the use of data in election campaigns respects privacy rights and upholds the integrity of the democratic process, more rules and transparency measures are required.

The way that social media companies handle political material and their part in halting the spread of disinformation have also drawn criticism. The information environment during political campaigns is significantly impacted by decisions made about content filtering, algorithmic biases, and platform restrictions. The necessity for free expression must be balanced with the duty to stop the spread of false or damaging information, which is a difficult task that requires constant communication and cooperation between platforms, governments, and civil society.

It is crucial to understand that a complete election campaign plan includes social media as only one element. Even if it presents special chances for outreach and participation, it should be accompanied by more conventional campaign strategies like neighborhood organization, town hall meetings, and face-to-face encounters with voters. The efficacy of a candidate's message may be maximized, and a wide variety of supporters can be mobilized, with a well-rounded campaign plan that integrates online and offline activities.

Social media and political campaigns have a nuanced and intricate interaction. Undoubtedly, social media has changed how politicians interact with constituents, garner support, and sway public opinion. But it also presents problems like false information, echo chambers, and privacy issues. Election campaigns may make the most of social media's potential to promote transparency, diversity, and significant democratic engagement by addressing these issues and using its advantages.

Chapter 5

Digital Governance

5. Introduction

The term "digital governance" describes the use of technology and digital tools to improve the effectiveness, accountability, and transparency of governance processes. It entails the use of digital technology in a number of governance-related processes, such as decision-making, service delivery, citizen engagement, and data management. By using technology, digital governance strives to enhance citizen service delivery, streamline government processes, and promote democratic decision-making.

The use of digital platforms for decision- and policy-making processes is one of the main components of digital governance. Governments may use these platforms to expedite decision-making procedures, collaborate with stakeholders, and gather and analyze data. Digital platforms, for instance, may be used to collect feedback from individuals via online surveys or crowdsourcing projects, enabling a more inclusive and participatory process for formulating policy. Advanced analytics technologies may also be used to evaluate vast amounts of data and provide insightful information to support evidence-based policy choices.

The digitalization of government services is a crucial aspect of digital governance. Governments may provide services to residents more effectively and efficiently by using digital technology. It is possible to create mobile and online portals that make it simple to use government services like paying taxes, requesting for licenses, or getting medical treatment. In addition to saving people time and effort, digitalization also improves service quality by reducing bureaucratic bottlenecks.

Digital governance also encourages accountability and openness in governmental activities. Governments may increase the openness of decision-making processes and increase public access to information by using digital technologies. Government data and information may be published in a standardized, machine-readable manner through open data initiatives, enabling people, academics, and companies to study and use the data for multiple reasons. improved public scrutiny of government acts is made possible by this improved openness, which also increases public confidence.

Digital governance must include citizen interaction. New ways for people to engage in politics, express their ideas, and influence decisions are made possible by digital technology. To include people in policy debates, solicit input on government efforts, and promote active participation in democratic processes, online platforms, social media, and e-participation technologies may be used.

By empowering individuals and allowing them to be heard, these digital platforms promote inclusive and representative government.

Cybersecurity and data management are important factors in digital governance. Governments must guarantee the security and ethical use of data given the growing dependence on digital technologies and data-driven decision-making. To preserve people' personal information and stop data breaches, effective data protection policies and frameworks should be in place. Governments must also spend money on cybersecurity infrastructure to guard against online attacks and guarantee the dependability and integrity of digital services.

A fundamental change in how governments function and interact with their constituents has been brought about by digital governance. Governments can improve service delivery, encourage openness and accountability, increase public involvement, and make better informed, evidence-based choices by using the promise of digital technology. The digital gap, data privacy issues, and cybersecurity dangers are just a few of the issues that digital governance also brings up and need to be addressed. However, digital governance has the potential to change government and provide more responsive, inclusive, and effective public administrations with careful design, investment, and cooperation.

5.1 E-Government and Digital Services

Governments now connect with residents, corporations, and other stakeholders in a different manner because to the strong instruments of e-government and digital services. Governments all over the globe have realized the potential of digitalization to enhance the effectiveness, transparency, and accessibility of public services as a result of the fast growth of technology and the extensive usage of the internet. The digitalization of several government operations, including service delivery, information distribution, and citizen engagement, has been made possible by this paradigm shift toward e-government.

E-government is fundamentally the process of providing individuals, companies, and government workers with services from the government via electronic methods. Online portals, mobile apps, digital payment systems, and electronic document management are just a few of the many activities that fall under this umbrella. E-government strives to improve user experience overall and expedite administrative procedures by using technology. On the other side, digital services include a wide range of online services and apps that governments provide to their citizens, allowing people to access and use public services more quickly and easily.

The ease that e-government and digital services provide to people is one of its main benefits. People may access a variety of government services from the comfort of their homes or workplaces through internet portals and mobile apps. By eliminating the need for in-person visits to government facilities, both residents and workers of the government may save time and effort. Online services are now available, offering a streamlined and user-friendly experience for tasks including enrolling for different programs, paying taxes, viewing public data, and applying for permits and licenses.

E-government also encourages accountability and openness in governance. The public has easier access to information thanks to the digitization of government procedures. A culture of transparency and well-informed decision-making is promoted by the ease with which citizens may obtain public data, reports, and regulations. Governments may also use digital platforms to spread information to a larger audience, aiding awareness-raising campaigns, policy announcements, and emergency warnings. This improved openness strengthens the democratic basis by increasing confidence between the government and its citizens.

E-government and digital services may improve service delivery while also saving governments a lot of money. Governments may save money on administrative expenses by switching from conventional paper-based systems to digital ones. These costs are related to paperwork, physical storage, and human processing. Government workers may concentrate on more difficult and strategic duties by automating the regular ones, which increases productivity. Digital services also make it possible for governments to gather, process, and use data more effectively, resulting in resource allocation and policy decisions that are supported by facts.

The empowerment of people via greater involvement and engagement is a vital component of e-government. Governments may use digital platforms to collect feedback, carry out surveys, and promote public discussions on a range of subjects. To ensure that policies and services are in line with their needs and ambitions, citizens may express their views, provide suggestions, and participate in decision-making processes. E-participation platforms also promote multi-stakeholder governance by encouraging cooperation between corporations, civil society groups, and governments.

However, there are a number of obstacles that must be overcome for e-government and digital services to be implemented successfully. Bridging the digital gap is a significant challenge since not all individuals have equal access to technology or the required digital literacy abilities. To guarantee inclusion and equitable access to digital services, governments must make investments in infrastructure development, encourage digital literacy initiatives, and assure accessible for disadvantaged areas. Since the digitalization of government procedures necessitates the capture and storage of enormous volumes of sensitive and personal data, privacy and data security are also major problems. To preserve citizen privacy, governments must prioritize effective data protection measures, set up secure systems, and pass laws.

Initiatives involving e-government have the potential to fundamentally alter how governments interact with their constituents. Governments may provide smooth and individualized experiences for those requesting public services via digital platforms. Instead of navigating several government agencies and offices, citizens may utilize a consolidated online portal that provides a wide variety of services. Citizens may do these chores with only a few clicks, whether they are applying for social benefits, renewing their driver's licenses, or making appointments with healthcare professionals.

Digital services are essential for fostering corporate development and economic prosperity. Governments may create websites that make it easier to register businesses and apply for licenses and permits. This simplified procedure promotes entrepreneurship and draws investment since it lowers administrative barriers and cuts down on the time and effort needed to launch a firm. Digital payment systems also make it simple for firms to meet their financial commitments to the government, such as tax payments and customs charges, improving efficiency and lowering the possibility of mistakes.

Furthermore, by reducing the environmental effect of conventional paper-based systems, e-government and digital services support sustainable development. Paper use, printing expenses, and energy usage are all greatly reduced as a result of the switch to digital procedures. Electronic document management solutions enable the safe and effective archiving, sharing, and retrieval of documents, hence minimizing the need for physical storage space and transit. These green practices encourage a more eco-friendly style of governance and are in line with the global goal for sustainable development.

Initiatives using e-government have the potential to improve interactions between companies and governments. Governments may provide companies access to useful data and resources, such market intelligence, regulatory updates, and financing possibilities, via digital platforms. This makes it easier for the public and private sectors to work together, encouraging innovation, economic development, and job creation. Additionally, digital services may help governments expedite the procurement process, facilitating private participation in public sector initiatives and government contracts.

E-government and digital services have shown to be beneficial in the fields of public safety and emergency management. Governments may use digital platforms to provide precise information in a timely manner during emergencies like public health crises and natural catastrophes. Residents have access to emergency response plans, notifications, and real-time information on medical facilities or evacuation routes. A quick and successful crisis response is made possible by the efficient coordination offered by digital communication channels between government organizations, first responders, and the general public.

Emerging concepts like artificial intelligence (AI), blockchain, and the Internet of Things (IoT) have the potential to improve e-government and digital services as technology continues to advance. Chatbots and virtual assistants powered by AI may provide people individualized support and assistance by responding to commonly asked queries, assisting them with procedures, and resolving problems in real-time. By guaranteeing the accuracy of records and enabling secure digital identities, blockchain technology may improve the security and transparency of government transactions. Governments may be able to gather data from a variety of sources, including smart sensors and devices, thanks to the Internet of Things (IoT), in order to enhance resource management, transportation, and urban planning.

Digital services and e-government have the potential to completely change how governments engage with their constituents, corporations, and other stakeholders. Governments may improve service delivery, encourage accountability and transparency, boost economic development, and increase public safety by embracing digital transformation. To guarantee the inclusion, trust, and effectiveness of e-government programs, governments must address issues including the digital gap, privacy concerns, and data security. Governments may use the benefits of e-government and digital services to build more effective, citizen-centered, and sustainable societies by using technology and innovation.

5.2 Smart Cities and Urban Planning

Urban planning and smart cities are essential elements in tackling the complicated issues brought on by the demand for sustainable development in the twenty-first century. Cities are under growing pressure to offer effective infrastructure, better services, and improved quality of life for their citizens as the world population continues to rise and relocate to metropolitan regions. In order to improve urban processes and make cities more livable, resilient, and sustainable, the idea of smart cities might be used in this situation.

ICT (information and communication technology) integration into different facets of urban life, such as transportation, energy, public safety, healthcare, and government, is at the center of smart city projects. Cities may gather, analyze, and use a ton of data by using the power of digital technology in order to obtain knowledge and make wise choices. With the help of this data-driven methodology, city planners may better allocate resources, organize business processes, and boost the effectiveness of urban systems as a whole.

Transportation is one of the important areas where smart cities and urban planning converge. Traffic jams and insufficient public transit systems have emerged as important issues for cities all over the globe as a result of the global surge in urbanization. Smart transportation options provide intriguing ways to deal with these problems. Cities may improve traffic flow, lessen congestion, and increase the effectiveness of public transit by combining intelligent transportation technologies, real-time traffic monitoring, and data analytics. Smart sensor technology and connectivity may also advance the development of driverless cars and encourage environmentally friendly forms of transportation like walking and cycling.

Another crucial component of smart cities and urban planning is energy management. Adopting smart grid technology may aid in optimizing energy distribution, reducing waste, and promoting renewable energy sources since cities use a substantial percentage of the world's energy. Cities may track trends of energy use, spot inefficiencies, and adopt focused measures for conservation and sustainability by using data analytics, smart meters, and sophisticated energy management systems. Additionally, the incorporation of smart infrastructure and buildings may lead to enhanced interior environmental quality, automated controls, and efficient energy use.

Urban regions' top priorities are public safety and security. In order to improve situational awareness, crime prevention, and emergency response skills, smart cities use cutting-edge surveillance systems, IoT devices, and data analytics. Cities may proactively identify crime hotspots, monitor population movements, and notice abnormalities by using real-time data streams, predictive analytics, and machine learning algorithms. Law enforcement organizations can properly manage their resources, react to crises quickly, and protect locals thanks to this proactive strategy.

Smart cities may significantly alter the healthcare and public health industries. Cities may increase access to healthcare, improve disease surveillance, and encourage preventative care by using telemedicine, remote patient monitoring, and wearable technology. Real-time health data may be gathered, analyzed, and shared to spot epidemics, identify trends in public health, and effectively allocate medical resources. Additionally, through boosting green areas, lowering pollution, and promoting active lives, smart city projects may concentrate on developing healthy and sustainable ecosystems.

Smart cities must have effective governance and public participation to succeed. Cities may promote openness, accountability, and cooperation through adopting open data programs, digital platforms, and participatory decision-making procedures. Urban development strategies may be shaped by citizens' access to real-time information, participation in policy debates, and feedback. Additionally, the delivery of e-government services, digital connection, and inclusive information access are made possible by smart city technology, bridging the digital gap and empowering neglected groups.

Smart cities and urban planning have a significant influence on environmental sustainability in addition to the aforementioned factors. Cities are essential in reducing the environmental effect of urbanization because of the growing awareness of climate change and the need to cut carbon emissions. The monitoring and improvement of water supplies, trash management, and energy usage are made possible by smart city technology.

Buildings that consume less energy, smart networks, and the incorporation of renewable energy all help to lower greenhouse gas emissions and advance sustainable development. Cities may optimize energy use, develop demand-response methods, and encourage the use of sustainable energy sources by leveraging sensors, data analytics, and automation. By doing this, cities become more robust to interruptions in the energy supply as well as contributing to the reduction of their carbon footprints.

The environmental sustainability initiatives of smart cities must also include waste management. Cities can optimize collection routes, monitor garbage levels in real-time, and promote recycling and composting by putting in place smart waste management systems. By allowing resource recovery and waste-to-energy conversion, these systems may decrease landfill utilization, lessen the environmental effect of waste disposal, and support a circular economy.

The management of water resources is essential to urban planning. Smart city technologies provide creative answers for effective water management in light of the issues posed by an aging water infrastructure and the growing shortage of freshwater. Leak detection, water quality monitoring, and irrigation system optimization are all possible with the help of smart sensors and monitoring systems. Additionally, data-driven insights may assist in the appropriate use of water resources by guiding water conservation efforts.

Quality of life and social connectedness are also impacted by the incorporation of smart city principles. Connectivity and digital technology help build thriving, diverse communities. Initiatives for "smart cities" put an emphasis on enhancing digital connection, offering free public WiFi, and encouraging digital literacy. By bridging the digital gap, these initiatives guarantee that all locals have equal access to knowledge and opportunity.

In addition, smart city technologies improve urban preparedness for crises and natural catastrophes. Cities may enhance their capacity for readiness, reaction, and recovery in the event of a catastrophe by combining sensor networks, early warning systems, and real-time data analysis. This entails keeping an eye on weather trends, foreseeing and controlling floods or earthquakes, and effectively coordinating emergency services. Smart city strategies allow for quick and precise reactions, saving lives and limiting damage in urgent circumstances.

For smart city efforts to be implemented successfully, urban planning is essential. It necessitates cooperation amongst many stakeholders, thorough understanding of the local environment, and the inclusion of public feedback. Urban planning that is done well takes into account the city's long-term goals while balancing social justice, environmental sustainability, economic growth, and cultural preservation. It entails developing mixed-use communities, effective transit networks, green areas, and open public places.

metropolitan planning and smart cities have the ability to completely change how metropolitan areas are created, developed, and managed. Cities may become more sustainable, resilient, and habitable through using technology, data, and public interaction. Numerous advantages result from the integration of smart city principles in the areas of transportation, energy, public safety, healthcare, environmental sustainability, and governance, including increased effectiveness, improved service delivery, and an improvement in the quality of life for locals. To build inclusive and people-centric cities for the future, it is vital to make sure that these programs promote privacy, security, and equality.

5.3 Blockchain and Distributed Ledger Technology

The breakthrough technologies of blockchain and distributed ledger technology (DLT) have the ability to reshape many different businesses and sectors. Fundamentally, blockchain and DLT provide safe, decentralized, and transparent platforms for storing and validating data.

The most well-known kind of DLT, blockchain, is simply a digital ledger that keeps track of transactions across several computers or network nodes. It works on the consensus concept, in which network users reach an understanding about the legitimacy of transactions using cryptographic techniques. Once a transaction has been verified, it is added to a block and connected to earlier blocks to create an immutable, tamper-proof chain of information.

Decentralization is one of the main characteristics of blockchain and DLT. Blockchain and DLT share the ledger across several participants or nodes, in contrast to conventional centralized systems, where the ledger is controlled by a single institution or authority. A copy of the full ledger is given to each participant, providing transparency and lowering the possibility of fraud or manipulation. Due to the decentralized nature, there is no longer any need for middlemen like banks or clearinghouses, which reduces costs and improves efficiency.

Transparency is a key component of blockchain and DLT. Anyone with network access may observe and validate transactions since the ledger is spread across several nodes. Since it becomes more difficult to edit or fabricate documents without being discovered, this openness increases confidence and accountability. It is especially helpful in sectors that need traceability, such supply chain management, where stakeholders can follow the flow of items and confirm their legitimacy.

The essential feature of blockchain and DLT is security. The security and tamper-proofness of transactions is ensured through the use of consensus processes and cryptographic algorithms. It is quite challenging to change or remove the data contained in a block after it has been added to the chain. The distributed structure of the ledger also makes it resistant to failures or assaults. Blockchain and DLT continue to operate as long as a sufficient number of nodes are active, unlike centralized systems where a single point of failure may bring the whole network to a halt.

DLT and blockchain technology have several uses. As decentralized digital currencies that provide safe and effective peer-to-peer transactions, cryptocurrencies like Bitcoin and Ethereum have grown in popularity in the financial sector. Smart contracts have the potential to revolutionize contract administration and simplify corporate procedures since they are programmable agreements that automatically execute when certain criteria are satisfied.

Another area where blockchain and DLT are making considerable progress is supply chain management. Stakeholders may guarantee transparency, authenticity, and accountability across the supply chain by tracking the flow of commodities from the point of origin to the point of destination on a blockchain. This technology may increase traceability, decrease the occurrence of counterfeit goods, and boost the effectiveness of logistical operations.

Blockchain and DLT are being investigated in sectors including healthcare, government services, energy, and intellectual property rights, in addition to finance and supply chain management. For instance, in the healthcare industry, patient records may be safely maintained on a blockchain, giving authorized doctors access to precise and current medical data. In order to increase transparency and lower fraud, governments are also looking at using blockchain for identity management, voting systems, and land registries.

Despite the many benefits that blockchain and DLT provide, there remain obstacles to be addressed. Some of the major obstacles that must be overcome for widespread adoption are scalability, energy consumption, and regulatory frameworks. Blockchain and DLT have the ability to revolutionize sectors, restructure workflows, and give people and companies more power via better efficiency, security, and trust as the technology develops and matures.

Blockchain and DLT have the potential to upend the realm of intellectual property rights in addition to the previous uses. A decentralized system for handling patents, copyrights, and trademarks may be developed using these technologies. It is simpler to establish ownership, monitor infringement, and streamline licensing arrangements when intellectual property assets are created, owned, and transferred on a blockchain. To the advantage of artists, inventors, and companies, this may substantially simplify and speed the process of securing and monetizing intellectual property.

Additionally, DLT and blockchain are being investigated for improving cybersecurity. Traditional centralized systems provide hackers a single point of access, making them susceptible to cyberattacks and data breaches. In contrast, since blockchain is decentralized, such assaults are less likely to succeed. Sensitive data may be safely stored and disseminated over a network by using cryptographic methods and distributed consensus procedures. This might improve data security, preserve individual privacy, and defend key infrastructure from online assaults.

Beyond cryptocurrencies, the financial industry is aggressively investigating the application of blockchain and DLT. The idea of decentralized finance (DeFi), which seeks to replicate conventional financial institutions like loans, insurance, and trading in a decentralized way using smart contracts, is one important breakthrough. By giving underprivileged communities access to financial services, decreasing dependence on conventional intermediaries, and facilitating peer-to-peer transactions with more transparency and cheaper costs, DeFi has the potential to expand financial inclusion.

The promise of blockchain and DLT is increasingly being recognized by governments and regulatory organizations. For public services like voting, land registration, and welfare distribution, several nations have begun testing blockchain-based solutions. Governments may increase voter confidence in the voting process, prevent corruption, and guarantee fair and accurate results by using the transparency and immutability of blockchain. Blockchain-based land registries may simplify real estate transactions, reduce legal wrangling, and stop fraud. Additionally, digital identities built on blockchain technology have the potential to give people control over their personal data, providing safe and quick access to public and private services.

The broad implementation of DLT and blockchain, however, confronts several difficulties. As the present blockchain infrastructure has constraints in terms of transaction speed and capacity, scalability continues to be a big challenge. To solve these problems, work is being done to provide scalable solutions including layer-two protocols and sharding methods. Another issue with certain consensus techniques, such proof-of-work, which need a lot of processing power, is energy usage. These issues may be reduced by switching to consensus processes that use less energy, such as proof-of-stake.

Additionally, the regulatory environment for blockchain and DLT is constantly developing. Initial coin offerings (ICOs), smart contracts, and cryptocurrencies are all treated differently by various authorities. To address issues with investor protection, anti-money laundering, tax compliance, and consumer rights without limiting innovation, governments and regulatory organizations must provide clear legal frameworks. To strike the appropriate balance and create an atmosphere where blockchain technology may flourish, cooperation between industry stakeholders and authorities is essential.

Blockchain and DLT have the power to completely change industries and the way information is recorded, validated, and shared. Numerous benefits in terms of security, effectiveness, and trust are provided by their decentralized and transparent structure. Blockchain and DLT are being investigated in a variety of fields, including banking and supply chain management, as well as healthcare, public services, and intellectual property. Although there are obstacles, continued research, technical progress, and legislative changes are laying the groundwork for widespread use and maximizing the promise of these ground-breaking innovations.

5.4 Open Data and Transparency

Modern government and social advancement depend on open data and transparency. The idea of making data freely accessible to the general public, without any limitations on access, consumption, or redistribution, is known as "open data." It entails exchanging numerous kinds of information in a machine-readable and intelligible manner, including public documents, scientific discoveries, statistical data, and more. On the other side, transparency refers to the openness, responsibility, and accessibility of data, procedures, and decision-making within businesses, governments, and society. Open data and transparency have the ability to increase efficiency, creativity, and trust across industries while enabling individuals to actively engage in reshaping their communities.

The idea that data produced or owned by public entities should be viewed as a priceless public asset is one of the key tenets of open data and transparency. Governments and organizations enable people, academics, businesspeople, and community organizations to access, examine, and use the data for diverse reasons by making it publicly accessible. Open data lays the groundwork for evidence-based decision-making, allowing individuals, academics, and politicians to better understand societal problems, spot patterns, and create solutions that work. By enabling people to keep tabs on and assess how well public institutions are doing, it also encourages accountability, resulting in improved effectiveness and reduced corruption.

Transparency and accessible data also support innovation and the expansion of the economy. When data is readily available, business owners and developers may use it to generate cutting-edge software, services, and goods. Open data programs promote entrepreneurship, job creation, and economic growth by fostering data-driven innovation. Open data may be used by organizations and startups to gather market insight, pinpoint consumer requirements, and create data-driven strategies. Because businesses may compare their performance to that of their competitors and pick up best practices, the availability of open data encourages competition and improves the standard of services.

Open data and transparency have a significant influence on public involvement and participation in democratic processes in addition to encouraging accountability and innovation. Citizens who have access to information are better able to comprehend and participate in governmental policies, budgets, and decision-making processes. Citizens may actively participate in governance, hold authorities responsible, and provide input on public services when they have access to government information. Governments, civil society groups, and people may work together more easily when there is access to open data, which promotes inclusive decision-making and the co-creation of solutions. Open data projects promote more inclusive and representative government by incorporating a wide variety of stakeholders in the process.

Open data and openness, it is crucial to highlight, sometimes present difficulties and need careful management. When making data publicly accessible, it is essential to guarantee data privacy and preserve sensitive information. The leaking of sensitive information that might endanger people or jeopardize national security should be prevented by safeguards. To make sure that open data is dependable, accurate, and useable across many platforms and applications, it is also important to focus on data quality and interoperability. To create common standards, formats, and protocols for data exchange, cooperation between organizations, governments, and technical specialists is crucial.

Governments and organizations must establish a comprehensive strategy in order to fully harness the promise of open data and transparency. They should provide precise guidelines and regulatory frameworks that encourage data disclosure and advance decision-making openness. Governments should aggressively share information, encourage public participation and awareness, and provide user-friendly platforms for gaining access to and using open data. Initiatives to create capacity may assist people and organizations in acquiring the abilities and information required to utilize open data efficiently. Governments, corporate companies, and civil society groups working together may spur the creation of novel solutions and guarantee the long-term viability of open data programs.

Transparency and open data are significant forces behind society advancement, responsibility, and innovation. Governments and organizations may promote trust, effectiveness, and public participation by making data openly accessible and encouraging openness in decision-making. Initiatives using open data let people make decisions based on facts, promote economic development and creativity, and provide people the ability to take part fully in political processes. To achieve ethical data sharing, issues like data privacy and quality must be resolved. Open data and transparency may unleash significant advantages for society and help create a more equitable and sustainable future with the correct policies, partnerships, and capacity-building initiatives.

5.5 Digital Divide and Inclusivity

The distance between people, groups, and civilizations who have access to digital technology like the internet and those who do not is referred to as the "digital divide." It includes differences in accessibility, cost, and computer literacy abilities. The digital gap presents substantial issues and exacerbates existing disparities in the rapidly connecting world of today, when the internet is essential for many parts of daily life.

Unfair access to technology is one of the main causes of the digital divide. In industrialized nations, access to the internet is increasingly commonplace and the vast majority of people have access to high-speed broadband connections. However, access is sometimes restricted in poor nations, especially in rural and isolated places. Due to a lack of infrastructure, people and communities are unable to take use of the many resources, opportunities, and information that are accessible online.

In addition, price poses a serious obstacle to digital inclusiveness. Despite recent decreases in price, many individuals still consider internet access to be a luxury, particularly those with lower incomes. Access to digital technology is further hampered by the high expenses involved in purchasing equipment like laptops or cellphones. As a consequence, it is very difficult for underprivileged groups and people to keep up with the fast changing digital world.

Another important component of the digital divide is digital literacy, or the capacity to utilize digital technology responsibly and effectively. Even if people have access to the internet, they may not have the skills to use it effectively, assess material critically, or safeguard their security and privacy. Because individuals who are already disadvantaged encounter more challenges in gaining the information and skills required to fully engage in the digital era, the digital skills gap exacerbates previously existing inequities.

The effects of the digital divide are widespread and have an effect on many areas of life, including civic involvement, work, healthcare, and education. Students who do not have access to the internet or digital gadgets, for instance, are significantly at a disadvantage compared to their counterparts who have. They could not have access to online learning materials, lose out on developing their digital abilities, and have difficulty keeping up with the demands of the job market for digital literacy. The difference in educational attainment between various groups is further widened as a result.

Similar to this, digital abilities are becoming more and more in demand across sectors in the workplace. Job seekers who lack digital literacy abilities are shut out of a variety of career options. The digital gap reinforces economic inequalities and restricts social mobility as digital technologies continue to impact the future of employment.

In addition, the digital divide affects results and access to healthcare. Accessing medical information and services is made simple and effective by telemedicine and online health platforms. However, those who lack internet connection or digital literacy are unable to take advantage of these developments, which results in inequities in the way healthcare is delivered and in health outcomes.

Building an equal and fair society requires addressing the digital gap and advancing digital inclusiveness. By investing in infrastructure development, guaranteeing affordable access to the internet, and offering digital skills training programs, governments, legislators, and organizations need to make closing the digital gap a top priority. Expanding connection may be greatly aided by public-private partnerships, especially in underprivileged regions.

All levels of education should include instruction in digital literacy to provide students with the knowledge and abilities necessary to succeed in the digital age. The gap in digital skills may be filled through programs aimed at improving computer literacy among underserved populations, such as low-income persons, elderly, and people with disabilities.

The demands and experiences of various communities must also be taken into account in attempts to improve digital inclusion. This entails creating intuitive digital user interfaces, taking accessibility guidelines into account, and overcoming linguistic and cultural hurdles. To create comprehensive solutions and guarantee that no one is left behind in the digital revolution, collaboration amongst stakeholders is crucial. This includes governments, technology corporations, organizations, and communities themselves.

In conclusion, in today's linked society, the digital divide poses a serious concern. The main causes of this inequality are access, price, and digital literacy. The effects on healthcare, employment, education, and general social inclusion are significant. However, we can close the gap and promote a more inclusive digital society by investing in infrastructure, encouraging affordability, and giving priority to digital literacy initiatives. To guarantee that everyone has equal chances and benefits from the revolutionary potential of technology, achieving digital inclusion needs cooperation, creativity, and a commitment to equality.

Chapter 6

Global Technopolitics

6. Introduction

The complex interaction between technology and politics on a worldwide scale is referred to as global technopolitics. It includes all the ways that global political systems, international relations, governance structures, and power dynamics are influenced and shaped by technology breakthroughs, innovation, and the digital transformation of society. Global technopolitics has become an important area of study in the linked world of today, when technology pervades almost every aspect of human existence.

The rapid development of information and communication technologies (ICTs) is one of the major forces behind global technopolitics. The ubiquity of the internet, social networking sites, and mobile devices has completely changed how people interact with one another, obtain information, and engage in public debate. These technology advancements have not only broadened the range of political participation but have also opened up new channels for political involvement, protest, and mobilization. Modern political landscapes have been significantly shaped by technology, from the Arab Spring revolutions to the Black Lives Matter movement.

Global technopolitics also takes into account how transnational businesses are influencing politics more and more. Technology behemoths like Google, Facebook, Amazon, and Alibaba have accumulated a lot of power and sway in both the political and economic spheres. They have sparked worries about privacy, spying, and the consolidation of power because to their capacity to gather enormous quantities of data, analyze user behavior, and influence public opinion. With discussions about antitrust laws, data security, and the role of social media platforms in disseminating disinformation and manipulation, the convergence between big tech and politics has grown in importance.

The development of automation and artificial intelligence (AI) has significant effects on world technopolitics. Automated trading systems, predictive policing, and face recognition technology are just a few examples of the decision-making processes that are increasingly using AI-driven algorithms. These changes present issues with transparency, accountability, and possible biases in algorithmic decision-making. In addition, socio-political effects of work automation and the replacement of human labor by machines include economic disparity and the necessity for new types of social protection.

Geopolitics of technology is also included in global technopolitics. A distinguishing aspect of the modern international order is the battle between states for technical superiority. Countries like the US and China are vying for the top spot in industries like quantum computing, artificial intelligence, 5G networks, and space exploration. This rivalry affects power dynamics, alliances, and geopolitical objectives in addition to its economic effects. It prompts questions about reliance on technology, national security, and the possibility of a fragmented global technological environment.

Global technopolitics also poses significant ethical and regulatory issues in addition to these dynamics. The creation of strong ethical and regulatory frameworks often lags behind the fast speed of technical advancement. International collaboration and governance systems are needed to address issues including data privacy, cybersecurity, autonomous weaponry, genetic engineering, and the effect of technology on human rights. Policymakers, academics, and civil society groups must ensure that technical breakthroughs are in line with moral standards and human values.

The intricate linkages between technology and politics in our linked world are included in global technopolitics. It deals with the ability of ICTs to reshape society, the sway of multinational businesses, the emergence of AI and automation, the geopolitics of technology, as well as the moral and legal issues they raise. Forgetting about and avoiding these processes would make it difficult to create a future in which technology is a force for good, democracy, and human welfare.

6.1 International Cooperation and Conflict

Global political scene fundamentally consists of two opposing forces: cooperation and conflict. Nations must negotiate intricate interactions with one another in an increasingly linked and interdependent world by balancing the pursuit of shared objectives and mutual benefits against conflicting interests and diametrically opposed ideologies. International cooperation is the term used to describe joint efforts made by nations to solve common problems, enhance global governance, and encourage peace and security. It includes a broad variety of activities, such as bilateral and multilateral organizations, international agreements, collaborative projects, and diplomatic engagements. The goal is to develop standards, guidelines, and structures that encourage collaboration and coordination, guarantee the peaceful settlement of disagreements, and promote the achievement of shared goals.

To address urgent global concerns including climate change, terrorism, pandemics, and poverty, international cooperation is crucial. Since these problems are interrelated, nations often band together to exchange information, pool resources, and coordinate solutions. For instance, virtually all countries came together under the Paris Climate Change Agreement to tackle the existential danger posed by global warming. Similar to this, the United Nations is crucial in promoting global cooperation by offering a forum for discussion, bargaining, and coordinated action.

Countries participate in trade agreements, economic partnerships, and financial aid programs as a form of economic cooperation. Regional trade blocs that foster economic integration, lower trade barriers, and advance prosperity for all members include the European Union and the Association of Southeast Asian Nations (ASEAN). Additionally, to help promote stability and growth, international financial organizations like the World Bank and the International Monetary Fund (IMF) provide money and expertise to needy nations.

Nevertheless, despite the inherent advantages of collaboration, disputes and tensions continue to exist on a global scale. States often have competing national interests, contrasting ideologies, and old grudges that may cause disagreements and even deadly conflicts. Territorial conflicts, resource access, ideological disagreements, violations of human rights, and rival spheres of influence may all lead to conflict.

Throughout history, there have been many conflicts across the globe, ranging from small-scale disagreements to major battles. These wars may have disastrous repercussions, including the loss of life, population relocation, economic downturns, and the deterioration of international relations. Conflict resolution calls for diplomatic efforts, talks, and sometimes the involvement of outside mediators. Regional authorities, non-governmental organizations, and international organizations like the United Nations Security Council all play important roles in conflict resolution and peacekeeping operations.

Conflicts may also affect people outside of the direct parties engaged in significant ways. They have the potential to undermine regional stability, heighten hostility between nations, and have repercussions for the world order. For instance, the Middle Eastern conflicts have had an impact on geopolitical dynamics, global oil markets, and refugee flows.

Conflict resolution and peacebuilding efforts take many different forms and include a range of strategies. Finding peaceful solutions requires the use of diplomacy, negotiation, and conversation as key instruments. Arbitration and mediation may aid in bridging gaps and encouraging compromise. Economic interconnectedness and the promotion of common values may also act as conflict resolution's accelerators. The protection of vulnerable people and maintenance of international norms, human rights principles, and humanitarian measures are essential.

There is a fine line between international collaboration and conflict, and this line is always shifting as new problems appear. Geopolitical disputes, nationalist movements, and technical breakthroughs have complicated the world scene in recent years. International cooperation has been hampered by the growth of populism and protectionism in certain nations, which has put existing norms and multilateral institutions to the test.

Nevertheless, in a world that is becoming more linked, international collaboration is still essential. The common problems that mankind faces, such as pandemics, climate change, and the pursuit of sustainable development, call for international cooperation and collective action. Countries may develop mutual trust, promote understanding, and create channels for peaceful conflict resolution via collaboration. Utilizing global collaboration while negotiating the intricacies of competing interests and ideologies is the key to creating a society that is more peaceful and wealthy.

6.2 Digital Diplomacy and Cyber Governance

International relations in the contemporary period now heavily rely on digital diplomacy and cyber governance. In order to handle the potential and problems given by the digital sphere, governments throughout the globe have realized the need of modifying their diplomatic tactics and governance structures. Digital diplomacy is the practice of governments conducting diplomatic operations, corresponding with foreign allies, and influencing public opinion internationally via the use of digital technology and online platforms. On the other side, cyber governance focuses on the creation and use of frameworks, rules, and policies to guarantee ethical conduct online and successfully handle cyber risks.

Online diplomacy, e-diplomacy, and public diplomacy in the digital era are only a few of the activities that fall under the umbrella of "digital diplomacy." To communicate with overseas audiences, advance their national interests, and project their soft power, governments use digital technologies including social media platforms, websites, and virtual conferencing. Through the use of digital diplomacy, diplomatic missions may create direct lines of contact with people, companies, and civil society groups on the other side of international boundaries. This open communication may increase mutual understanding, trust, and collaboration between countries. Additionally, digital diplomacy offers a platform for quick and efficient diplomacy by enabling countries to quickly react to crises, distribute information, and build narratives in real-time.

Governments must build complete plans that complement their foreign policy goals in order to participate in digital diplomacy successfully. These tactics have to include explicit rules for using social media, producing content, and interacting with online communities. To understand the digital world, participate in public diplomacy initiatives, and handle possible diplomatic snags brought on by online encounters, diplomatic employees need training and expertise. To maintain uniform message, prevent misunderstandings, and increase the effect of digital diplomacy activities, cooperation between diplomatic missions, foreign ministries, and key stakeholders is essential.

Cyber governance is essential in handling the problems brought on by the digital environment, along with digital diplomacy. The creation of legal, regulatory, and technological frameworks for cyber governance includes regulating cyberspace, safeguarding vital infrastructure, and reducing cyberthreats. It covers topics including cybersecurity, data protection, privacy, international collaboration, and online conduct standards. For the digital world to remain stable, trustworthy, and confident as well as to defend national security and uphold people's rights and freedoms, effective cyber governance is necessary.

Both internal and international collaboration are necessary for cyber governance. Governments must set up strong legal and regulatory frameworks at the national level to deal with cyberthreats, safeguard key infrastructure, and advance cybersecurity awareness and education. In order to create novel solutions and exchange best practices, collaboration between the public and private sectors is essential. Governments work diplomatically to negotiate and set standards of appropriate conduct in cyberspace. In order to handle global cyber issues, multilateral institutions like the United governments play a vital role in promoting communication and collaboration between governments.

Addressing the problem of cyberwarfare and state-sponsored cyberattacks is a crucial component of cyber governance. In order to prevent and stop hostile cyber activity, governments must establish laws and standards as cyber capabilities advance. The use of diplomatic channels, international accords, and bilateral collaboration are essential for lowering the likelihood of an attack's escalation and discovering who is responsible. To build a more secure and reliable digital environment, procedures for information exchange, incident response, and attribution must be developed.

Cyber governance and digital diplomacy are essential facets of modern international relations. The rapid development of technology has changed how countries interact and combat cyberthreats. Through the use of digital diplomacy, governments may communicate with international audiences, project their soft power, and instantly react to crises on a global scale. On the other side, cyber governance focuses on creating frameworks, rules, and regulations to control cyberspace, safeguard vital infrastructure, and encourage ethical conduct. To harness the advantages of the digital era while lowering its hazards, collaboration is required on both a national and worldwide level.

6.3 Data Localization and National Sovereignty

Data localization is the practice of mandating that data be processed and kept in a certain geographic area, usually inside the boundaries of a given nation. As governments and politicians struggle with the convergence of technology, data, and national sovereignty, this idea has attracted a lot of attention recently.

National sovereignty is the capacity and independence of a country to rule itself free from outside influence. It includes the capacity to make choices and adopt legislation that are in the interests of the state and its people. Data is essential to society in the digital era for many reasons, including the economy, national security, and privacy. As a consequence, nations are attempting to establish their sovereignty over data transfers that occur inside their borders more often.

Data localization proponents contend that it is essential for maintaining cultural values, fostering economic progress, and safeguarding national security. Data localization may aid in preventing illegal access and data breaches by foreign organizations from the standpoint of national security. Governments may have more control over sensitive information, such as secret government data or crucial infrastructure systems, by requiring that it be kept and processed domestically. In a globalized environment, sustaining sovereignty and protecting national interests are considered as being dependent on this control.

Data localization proponents also contend that it fosters entrepreneurship and economic development. Governments may guarantee that domestic businesses have access to vital data by mandating local data storage, which encourages innovation and entrepreneurship. In addition to generating employment possibilities, data localisation regulations may encourage investment in data centers and associated infrastructure. Additionally, supporters contend that data localization may stop foreign businesses from abusing data, ensuring that the economic gains from data stay domestically.

Another argument in favor of data localisation is cultural preservation. Some nations want to preserve control over how data is handled and used because they regard data as a reflection of their cultural identities. They contend that data localization may safeguard regional customs, values, and languages and avoid the domination of outside cultural forces. Governments may control material and make sure that it adheres to their cultural and social values by retaining data domestically.

Data localization has detractors, meanwhile, who express worry about any possible drawbacks. Data localization policies, according to their critics, may stunt innovation and economic progress by splintering the global digital economy. Global commerce has been enabled and the expansion of multinational corporations has been driven by the unrestricted movement of data across borders. Limiting data flows via localization regulations may make it more difficult for enterprises to reach markets and deter foreign direct investment.

Data localisation may compromise privacy and data security, according to critics. Governments may sometimes employ data localization as a surveillance tool to get more access to the private information of residents. Data kept inside a nation's boundaries can be covered by less severe privacy laws or monitoring, thus putting people at higher risk for privacy breaches. Additionally, data localisation might erect obstacles to international law enforcement and cybersecurity collaboration, making it more difficult to fight transnational crimes and cyberthreats.

Data localisation may also result in higher expenses for enterprises. It may be time-consuming and costly to maintain local data storage infrastructure and adhere to varied data localization regulations in multiple nations. Particularly small and medium-sized businesses could find it difficult to achieve these standards, which would restrict their capacity to compete in international markets.

It is a difficult undertaking to strike a balance between data localisation and the concepts of national sovereignty. Data localization regulations should be carefully evaluated by governments, taking into consideration aspects like national security, economic growth, privacy, and international collaboration. To guarantee that data localization policies do not jeopardize the core tenets of an open and interconnected digital world while simultaneously respecting a country's ability to defend its interests and exercise its sovereignty, the proper balance must be struck.

The influence on cross-border data flows and global commerce is a crucial component of the discussion around data localization and national sovereignty. Data has grown to be a valuable resource that drives the global digital economy in a connected world. A lot of sectors, like e-commerce, cloud computing, and financial services, depend on the capacity to move data easily across international boundaries. These sectors may be affected, and commerce between countries may be hampered, by restrictions on data flows caused by localization regulations.

By collaborating and sharing information, companies have been able to extend their operations, reach clients in faraway areas, and promote innovation. Countries run the danger of cutting themselves off from the advantages of a worldwide digital economy by enforcing data localization laws. Particularly smaller economies could struggle to draw foreign investment and fully participate in the global economy.

Additionally, data localisation strategies may cause the internet to become more dispersed. Users have historically been able to access information from anywhere in the globe because to the internet's history as a borderless network. Data localization has the potential to weaken the internet's global character and give rise to distinct digital universes with their own sets of laws. This fragmentation may restrict the possibilities for a genuinely global digital society by impeding communication and cooperation, as well as the free flow of information.

The problems caused by data localisation and national sovereignty are greatly helped by international frameworks and agreements. World Trade Organization (WTO) and World Intellectual Property Organization (WIPO) are two organizations that have been trying to create rules and regulations that balance national interests while fostering the free movement of information. These agreements seek to set common guidelines and requirements for cybersecurity, data protection, and privacy, guaranteeing that countries may maintain their sovereignty while yet benefiting from international data flows.

Multilateral agreements on data localisation may also make it easier to work together on issues like intellectual property rights, cybersecurity, and law enforcement. Countries may address concerns about national security without using stringent localization restrictions that can have unintended implications by developing frameworks for data exchange and mutual trust.

In the digital era, data localisation and national sovereignty are intricately intertwined notions. Data localization initiatives may be motivated by important considerations like national security, economic growth, and cultural preservation, but they also bring up serious issues with respect to privacy, global commerce, and internet accessibility. The establishment of international frameworks that allow nations to express their sovereignty without cutting themselves off from the global digital ecosystem is necessary to strike the correct balance, as is careful assessment of the possible advantages and costs.

6.4 Global Trade and Technological Innovation

In today's linked world, international commerce and technology innovation are now deeply entwined. Technology's quick development has altered commercial practices and had a significant influence on trade patterns throughout the world. Digital platforms' rise, the Internet of Things' (IoT), artificial intelligence's (AI) development, and other technology advancements have opened up new trade opportunities and produced a global market that transcends national boundaries.

The nature of international commerce has changed significantly as a result of technological progress. It has lowered obstacles and made it possible for companies to enter new markets by facilitating the efficient flow of products, services, and money across international boundaries. E-commerce platforms have become effective tools for companies, enabling them to access clients throughout the globe and streamlining international trade. As a result, there has been a huge growth in global commerce, with small and medium-sized businesses (SMEs) particularly benefitting from easier access to markets throughout the world.

In addition, supply networks and logistics have changed as a result of technology improvements. Production procedures have been enhanced through automation and robots, which has led to higher output and lower costs. Smart technology application has improved supply chain visibility, allowing companies to track and optimize the flow of commodities throughout the world. Examples of these technologies include sensors and tracking devices. This has sped up deliveries, decreased the cost of maintaining inventories, and increased overall trade efficiency.

Technology has also made it easier to share information and ideas, encouraging worldwide cooperation and creativity. Digital communication technologies have facilitated the flow of knowledge and promoted the development of international innovation networks by making it simpler for companies to communicate with partners, suppliers, and clients on a worldwide scale. As a consequence, new concepts and technology may spread quickly, resulting in the creation of ground-breaking goods and services that stimulate international commerce.

Additionally, technological innovation has spawned new sectors and business models, opening doors for economic expansion and employment creation. For instance, the emergence of collaborative consumption has been made possible by the sharing economy, which is driven by digital platforms. Companies like Uber and Airbnb, which employ technology to link people with underused resources, have changed the transportation and lodging industries, respectively. These innovative company strategies have increased commerce while also generating new job possibilities and advancing the economy.

Global commerce and technical advancement, however, often provide difficulties and worries. The discrepancy in access to and acceptance of technology between rich and poor nations is known as the "digital divide," which is a significant problem. Unfair access to technology may make already existing disparities worse and make it more difficult for certain nations to participate in international commerce. Promoting sustainable and fair global commerce requires bridging this gap and guaranteeing inclusive technical innovation.

Another issue is the possibility for conventional sectors to be disrupted and for employees to be displaced as a result of technology improvements. Technology not only opens up new possibilities, but it also makes certain employment obsolete. Governments and corporations must invest in upskilling and retraining programs to provide people the skills they need in the digital age. In the context of international commerce and technological innovation, legislation and regulations must also be in place to guarantee fair competition, safeguard consumer rights, and address concerns about privacy and data security.

Global commerce and technical advancement are intricately linked and mutually supportive. Modern technology has revolutionized business practices by opening up new markets, simplifying supply chains, encouraging innovation, and spawning new industries. However, issues like the digital divide and workforce relocation need focus and preventative action. Countries may use the potential of international commerce to generate economic growth, advance sustainable development, and enhance the general well-being of people by embracing technological innovation and tackling these issues.

6.5 Technological Hegemony and Power Dynamics

The domination and control over the creation, manufacturing, and use of technology exercised by a certain group, nation, or organization is referred to as technological hegemony. It deals with the uneven distribution of power and resources in the technological sphere, which causes imbalances in the dynamics of world power. This idea emphasizes how cutting-edge innovation and technology may be used as instruments to maintain current power systems and serve the interests of those in charge.

A key factor in determining technological predominance is power dynamics. Technology development and acquisition have always been strongly correlated with economic and military strength. Technological development gives dominating players the opportunity to maintain or grow their influence while restricting the progression of others. Stronger governments or firms are able to impose global trade and investment rules, manage intellectual property rights, and influence technology norms.

The concentration of research and development activity in a few prominent areas or institutions is one sign of technological hegemony. The ability to spend extensively in infrastructure, technological innovation, and scientific research gives countries or organizations with large resources and capacities an edge over less developed areas. Inequalities in power may persist as a result of this resource concentration as less powerful players struggle to keep up with the technological environment's fast evolution.

Furthermore, technical hegemony includes market control and production in addition to the development stage. Advanced economies often have the means and know-how necessary to produce and disseminate technologies on a big scale. They may use their dominating position to define industry standards, manage global supply chains, and affect market pricing. Their position of power is strengthened by this control, which enables them to reap financial rewards and influence game rules.

Data and information are another area where power dynamics are evident. Data has grown to be a significant resource in the digital era that may be used for social, political, and economic objectives. Large data sets and sophisticated analytical tools may help users obtain important insights and exert influence over a variety of sectors. The power of dominating players is further increased by their control over data collection, storage, and analysis, which gives them the ability to sway narratives, sway public opinion, and sway decision-making processes.

Power dynamics and technological hegemony present issues of equality, fairness, and the possibility for exploitation. Less powerful actors may come to rely on dominating forces for access to necessary technology, losing their independence and their ability to choose their own growth routes. Furthermore, the power and influence held by strong players may cause certain groups or areas to be marginalized or excluded, which would exacerbate already-existing social, economic, and political imbalances.

The systems that now support disparities must be identified and challenged in order to address technological hegemony and power dynamics. Between dominant and disadvantaged players, encouraging cooperation, information exchange, and technology transfer may help close the gap. A more equal distribution of technical skills may be encouraged by funding R&D projects in underrepresented areas and fostering inclusive innovation ecosystems.

To solve the issues brought on by technological hegemony, international collaboration and the creation of open, inclusive governance structures are crucial. To level the playing field and lessen the concentration of power, norms, standards, and legislation that encourage fair competition, defend intellectual property rights, and protect data privacy should be developed. A more equitable and inclusive world order may be achieved through empowering people, communities, and countries to actively engage in determining the course of technology developments.

The uneven distribution of power and resources in the field of technology is highlighted by the interplay between technical hegemony and power dynamics. Control over the creation, production, and dissemination of technology has the potential to strengthen existing power structures, maintain disparities, and restrict the agency of less powerful actors. In order to overcome these obstacles, coordinated efforts must be made to advance fair access to technology, support inclusive innovation ecosystems, and develop open governance frameworks. To manage the intricacies of power relations and work toward a more just and sustainable future, it is possible to question the existing quo and advocate for a more inclusive and balanced approach to technology.

Chapter 7

Ethical Considerations in Technopolitics

7. Introduction

Technopolitical ethics takes into account the intricate interactions between technology and political systems, emphasizing the moral conundrums and obligations that emerge in this changing environment. It is increasingly important to examine and address the ethical issues raised by the use of technology as it continues to mold and affect our democratic institutions. The numerous facets of ethical issues in technopolitics will be covered in this paragraph, including privacy, data governance, algorithmic bias, digital rights, and transparency.

In technopolitics, privacy is a crucial ethical problem. Advanced surveillance technologies have made it possible for governments and businesses to gather enormous quantities of personal data, generating worries about surveillance capitalism and the deterioration of human privacy. As governments use technical tools for intelligence collection and counterterrorism, striking a balance between security and privacy becomes more important. In order to preserve individual rights, ethical concerns dictate that the gathering and use of personal data be controlled by explicit norms that provide permission, purpose restriction, and data reduction.

In technopolitics, data administration presents additional ethical difficulties. It's possible that the growing dependence on data-driven decision-making techniques could exacerbate existing power disparities and support prejudice. For instance, algorithmic bias happens when automated systems reproduce and maintain the biases existing in the data they are trained on, resulting in unjust results. Algorithmic accountability and transparency are required by ethical concerns, and bias detection and mitigation methods must be in place. To avoid amplifying current social injustices, it is also essential to ensure diverse participation in the development and deployment of technology.

In technopolitics, digital rights become an important ethical issue. Access to digital tools and platforms is becoming more important for democratic engagement as technology becomes more pervasive in political processes. A power imbalance caused by the digital gap, in which certain groups lack access to technology, prevents equal political participation. In order to provide equitable access and digital literacy for all people, initiatives to close this gap are required by ethical concerns. In addition, it's crucial to defend free speech, stop online abuse, and avoid censorship in order to secure digital rights.

In technopolitics, accountability and transparency are fundamental ethical ideals. Concerns about undue influence, manipulation, and disinformation are raised by the opaqueness of the algorithms and decision-making procedures employed in political campaigns and administration. The techniques used to gather and analyze data, how algorithms work, and the standards utilized in automated decision-making must all be made known to the public. Governments and tech corporations must be transparent in order for people to understand and evaluate the systems that affect their lives, which is required by ethical concerns.

Furthermore, the creation of ethical norms and legislation often lags behind the rapid speed of technical change. As a result, technopolitical ethics must be approached with initiative. Technology developers, politicians, ethicists, and members of civil society must work together in interdisciplinary teams to include ethical issues into the design and implementation of innovations from the beginning. Similar to environmental effect assessments, ethical impact analyses may aid in identifying possible ethical issues and direct the ethical development and use of technology in political situations.

A broad variety of issues are covered by ethical considerations in technopolitics, including privacy, data governance, algorithmic bias, digital rights, transparency, and proactive ethical frameworks. To create a just and equitable technopolitical environment, it is essential to balance the advantages of technology breakthroughs with the possible threats and moral quandaries they may provide. Societies may negotiate the difficulties presented by technology while sustaining moral standards in political decision-making processes by stressing individual rights, inclusion, transparency, and accountability.

7.1 Algorithmic Bias and Fairness

When algorithms, driven by artificial intelligence (AI), create biased results or reinforce preexisting prejudices in data, this practice of systematic and unfair discrimination is referred to as algorithmic bias. It is critical to address the problem of algorithmic bias and assure fairness in the results of AI systems as they come to play in more and more areas of our life, such as job choices, loan approvals, and criminal justice.

Many things may lead to algorithmic bias. Biased data used to train the algorithms is one major cause. Unfair results may result if the training data is biased or not representative, since the algorithm may learn to reinforce such biases. A recruiting algorithm could unintentionally prejudice against certain groups in the hiring process, for instance, if the historical data used to train it shows gender or racial bias.

The design decisions made during the construction of the algorithm are another source of bias. The weighting given to various factors or the characteristics chosen might bring bias into the algorithm. For instance, if an algorithm used to assess creditworthiness takes into account variables that serve as proxies for race, such zip codes or educational attainment, it may provide biased results.

The optimization techniques employed in machine learning might also generate bias. Algorithms are often improved to reduce mistakes or increase accuracy, however this might result in inconsistent results for various groups. The algorithm may perform better on majority groups and perform worse on minority groups, perpetuating existing inequities, if the training data is unbalanced or some groups are underrepresented.

Fairness must be promoted as algorithmic bias is addressed, which calls for a multifaceted strategy. First and foremost, it is essential to guarantee that the training data is impartial and representative. To find and correct any biases that may be present, thorough data collection, preparation, and validation are required. Additionally, diverse development teams with a range of viewpoints and experiences may aid in identifying and minimizing biases throughout the algorithm development process.

In order to combat algorithmic bias, transparency and interpretability are also critical. In order to help consumers and stakeholders understand how choices are produced and spot possible biases, algorithms should be explicable. This may include using interpretable models, offering justifications for choices, or establishing guidelines for openness and accountability.

To find and fix biases, algorithms must also undergo regular audits and reviews. Continuous observation may aid in spotting biased results and provide chances for algorithmic advancement. To guarantee fairness and avoid differential effects on protected groups, evaluations should be undertaken across a variety of demographic groupings.

The importance of legal and regulatory frameworks in promoting fairness and preventing algorithmic bias is crucial. Governments and organizations should create policies and rules that support equality, responsibility, and openness in AI systems. To guarantee that algorithms are created and used in an ethical and impartial way, these frameworks should cover concerns like data protection, privacy, and the responsible use of AI.

Finally, in order to combat algorithmic prejudice, public awareness and education are essential. Promoting awareness of the limits and inherent biases of AI systems may enable people to recognize and object to unjust results. Society can work together to reduce algorithmic bias and create more equal systems by promoting a culture of responsible AI usage and fighting for justice.

To guarantee justice and equality in the use of AI systems, algorithmic bias is a critical problem that must be addressed. We can lessen the effects of algorithmic bias and work to develop AI systems that uphold the principles of fairness and justice for all by addressing biases in data, design, and optimization, promoting transparency, carrying out regular evaluations, implementing regulatory frameworks, and increasing public awareness.

7.2 Data Privacy and Protection

The digital world in which we live places a premium on data privacy and protection. The need of protecting personal information has increased due to the fast development of technology and the growing dependence on digital platforms. Data privacy refers to a person's right to manage their personal information, including deciding who has access to it and how it will be used. In contrast, data protection entails taking steps to stop illegal access to, use of, or disclosure of personal data.

In the linked world of today, several institutions, including corporations, government agencies, and internet platforms, continuously gather, retain, and exchange personal data. Sensitive information including names, addresses, financial information, and even biometric information may be included in this data. To meet the necessity for securing people' personal information and ensuring that corporations handle data responsibly, data privacy policies and legislation have evolved.

The General Data Protection Regulation (GDPR), which was put into effect by the European Union (EU) in 2018, is one of the most prominent laws in this area. With the GDPR, a framework for data protection is established, allowing people more control over their personal data and forcing businesses to treat it securely. It establishes harsh penalties for non-compliance and requires informed permission for data gathering. It also gives people the right to view and correct their personal information.

Many nations outside of the EU have passed their own rules governing data protection and privacy. For instance, in the United States, the California Consumer Privacy Act (CCPA) gives customers the right to know what personally identifiable information is being gathered about them and gives them the option to refuse its sale. The Personal Data Protection Bill in India, which also addresses consent and individual rights, intends to control the gathering, archiving, and processing of personal data.

Organizations themselves must take proactive measures to secure data privacy and protection in addition to following regulatory requirements. This involves putting in place strong security mechanisms, such firewalls and encryption, to protect data from unwanted access. Regular audits and assessments may assist find weaknesses and guarantee that privacy laws are being followed.

Additionally, data security and privacy go beyond legal compliance. When managing personal data, corporations must show openness, accountability, and appropriate data procedures. This raises ethical issues. To let people know how their data is being gathered, used, and shared, privacy rules should be accessible and written in plain language. Additionally, organizations should set up protocols for data breaches, including prompt notification of impacted parties and the appropriate authorities.

Artificial intelligence (AI) and machine learning are two examples of recent technological developments that provide new problems for data privacy and security. In order to train and improve algorithms, these technologies often depend on enormous volumes of data, which raises questions regarding data anonymization and possible re-identification of people. It's critical to strike a balance between using data for innovation and preserving individual privacy.

The Internet of Things (IoT) and wearable technology are two more developing technologies that produce a ton of personal data. It becomes crucial to ensure that data is gathered and maintained safely and that people are informed of how their data is being used. Organizations should include privacy concerns into the design of their goods and services from the beginning, according to the privacy-by-design principles.

Governments and regulatory organizations have a critical part in data privacy and protection as well, so it's not only a matter of personal responsibility. To handle new privacy problems and stay up with technological changes, they must constantly adapt and update their policies. Establishing thorough frameworks that protect personal data while promoting innovation and economic progress requires cooperation amongst stakeholders, including legislators, organizations, and people.

The safety and privacy of personal data are crucial components of the digital era. Individuals must have control over their information as a result of the growing gathering and use of personal data, and businesses must manage data ethically and securely. In order to protect privacy rights, laws like the GDPR and CCPA have been enacted, and businesses are required to have strong security measures and ethical standards in place. It's critical to strike a balance between technology advancement and privacy, and continuing cooperation between stakeholders is required to meet new difficulties. In the end, sustaining trust and defending individual rights in our networked society depend on data privacy and protection.

7.3 Autonomous Systems and Responsibility

Innovative technical developments like autonomous systems have the potential to completely transform many different businesses and facets of daily life. These systems, which often use machine learning and artificial intelligence (AI) algorithms, are made to carry out activities and make choices without the involvement of a person. Autonomous systems are gradually becoming a part of our everyday lives, from self-driving vehicles and drones to robotic helpers and intelligent virtual agents.

The idea of responsibility is a crucial factor to take into account when it comes to autonomous systems. Due of the degree of autonomy these systems possess, concerns have been raised about who should be responsible for their choices and any possible negative effects. The dispersed nature of responsibility in autonomous systems presents particular difficulties in contrast to conventional human-operated systems, where ownership of responsibility normally rests with the human operator.

Functional responsibility and moral responsibility are the two basic categories into which responsibility in autonomous systems may be divided. Functional accountability deals with the system's efficiency and dependability on a technological level. It includes things like making sure the system works as intended, complies with safety regulations, and performs within predetermined limits. In this context, accountability often lies with the creators, implementers, and users of autonomous systems who are in charge of assuring their appropriate operation and upkeep.

The ethical implications of autonomous systems' choices and acts, on the other hand, are covered under the concept of moral responsibility. As these systems develop, they can come into circumstances that call for moral decisions, such as selecting between alternative courses of action that might have moral repercussions. The absence of a conscious agent making choices makes assigning moral culpability difficult. However, many parties engaged in the design and implementation of the system may be held accountable.

Emphasizing the need of human monitoring and decision-making is one way to deal with the problem of moral responsibility in autonomous systems. Engineers and designers may include components that enable human operators to keep an eye on the system's operations and take appropriate action as required. The goal of this strategy, known as "human-in-the-loop," is to balance the advantages of autonomous systems with the need for human oversight and responsibility.

The idea of communal responsibility is one viewpoint on accountability in autonomous systems. Collective accountability acknowledges that the development, deployment, and usage of autonomous systems include a network of stakeholders, including manufacturers, politicians, regulators, and end-users rather than placing blame on a single person or organization. Each member of this network has a responsibility to contribute to the responsible design, implementation, and governance of autonomous systems.

The establishment of clear legal and regulatory frameworks is essential to ensuring the appropriate conduct of autonomous systems. Standards and requirements for autonomous systems, such as those governing data privacy, safety, and responsibility, should be outlined in these frameworks. In order to safeguard the rights of people and the interests of society as a whole, governments and regulatory agencies play a critical role in developing and enforcing these frameworks.

To address the social and ethical effects of autonomous systems, academic, industrial, and policymaker cooperation and continuing study are essential. The creation of standards and best practices for responsible AI and autonomous system development that take ethical issues into account from the very beginning of system design may be aided by multidisciplinary talks and efforts.

The development of autonomous systems presents both enormous potential and difficulties, especially in terms of accountability. In autonomous systems, accountability may be divided into two categories: moral and functional. The former deals with the moral ramifications of the latter's behavior. A comprehensive strategy incorporating stakeholders from the development, deployment, and governance phases is needed for responsibility allocation in these systems. The appropriate and ethical integration of autonomous systems into our everyday lives is something society may work toward via a mix of human monitoring, legal frameworks, and cooperative initiatives.

7.4 Human Enhancement and Bioethics

The use of technical developments to increase human capacities beyond their inherent constraints is referred to as "human enhancement." It combines a number of disciplines, including biotechnology, neurology, genetics, and information technology, with the goal of enhancing physical, mental, and emotional qualities. While the promise for increasing quality of life and expanding human potential is enormous, human augmentation also poses significant bioethical issues that must be carefully considered.

Fairness and equality are two of the major bioethical issues regarding human augmentation. It may increase current societal inequities and create a split between enhanced and non-enhanced people if particular persons or groups get access to enhancement technologies that provide them considerable benefits. This may result in a dystopian situation where a wealthy elite rules society and the rest are left behind. Thus, maintaining a fair and inclusive society requires guaranteeing equal distribution and access to human improvement technology.

The ideas of autonomy and personal identity are the subject of another ethical issue. Technologies for human improvement have the power to fundamentally change a person's physical and mental capabilities. This calls into doubt the veracity of individual accomplishments and the maintenance of individual identity. The sense of self and personal autonomy of an individual may be compromised if enhancements are utilized to change their characteristics or skills in order to meet society standards or expectations. A significant ethical dilemma arises when trying to maintain uniqueness while improving human skills.

Additionally, it is important to carefully consider the security and long-term effects of human augmentation technology. Genetic and biotechnological developments have exciting possibilities, but they also carry certain hazards and unknowns. The employment of enhancement methods may have unexpected repercussions, such as unanticipated health issues or unintentional genetic alterations. Therefore, to reduce possible damage and guarantee the safety of people undergoing enhancement operations, rigorous scientific study, extensive risk assessment, and complete regulation are required.

Beyond the personal level to social and global dimensions, human augmentation has ethical ramifications. The quest for improvement could result in a combative "arms race," in which countries or people compete to exceed one another by using ever-more-advanced technology. This raises questions about the militarization of human enhancement and the possibility of producing sportsmen or warriors that are on par with superhuman strength. Additionally, there may be new types of inequality across countries because to the discrepancies in access to augmentation technologies around the world.

Considerations of human dignity and the natural order are also included in the ethical discussion around human augmentation. The essential dignity and worth of human existence, according to critics, are undermined by meddling with human nature and unnaturally boosting our capacities. They contend that adopting enhancement technology might result in a reductionist view of people, where people are seen as nothing more than tools for manipulation and development. Important ethical issues that must be carefully balanced against the possible advantages of human enhancement include the respect for human dignity and the preservation of the natural order.

Bioethics is essential in navigating the complicated world of human improvement by offering moral frameworks and rules. To make sure that the creation and use of enhancement technologies are consistent with moral standards and social norms, it is necessary for scientists, philosophers, legislators, and the general public to work together across disciplines. The ethical issues and possible negative effects related to human improvement must be addressed in open and inclusive dialogues that encourage a process of decision-making that considers many points of view.

The potential for human improvement to improve human existence, expand our capacities, and go above mental and physical constraints is enormous. To guarantee the appropriate and ethical development and use of enhancement technologies, it is essential to address the bioethical issues concerning justice, autonomy, safety, social effect, human dignity, and the natural order. We may work to exploit the advantages of human improvement while defending the values and ideals that characterize our common humanity by adopting a deliberate and inclusive approach.

A broad variety of technology interventions aiming at enhancing many facets of human life are included in the multidimensional idea of human augmentation. It encompasses both cognitive and physical improvements, such as better memory, focus, or problem-solving skills. Physical improvements include enhanced strength, stamina, or sensory awareness. It also includes psychological improvements including resilience, emotional intelligence, and mood control.

Incredibly significant developments in the realm of human improvement have been made possible by developments in biotechnology, genetics, and information technology. For instance, genetic engineering methods like CRISPR-Cas9 have the ability to alter the human genome, making it possible to fix hereditary illnesses or improve desirable features. Brain-computer interfaces have the potential to improve cognitive capacities, and neuroprosthetic devices have been created to help paralyzed people regain their movement activities.

Human improvement has great potential, but it also poses challenging ethical issues that need careful consideration. One of the main issues is what is considered "normal" or "natural." Human augmentation, according to critics, contradicts the inherent worth of human nature and upsets the natural order of things. They argue that going beyond what is deemed normal in terms of modifying human characteristics might result in a loss of authenticity and make it difficult to distinguish between what is real and what has been artificially altered.

Furthermore, a significant problem in the field of human improvement is the possibility of societal injustice and prejudice. Access to enhancement technologies is likely to be restricted to people with financial resources or social status, particularly in its early phases. As a result, there may be an increase in already existing inequities since enhanced people may have a major advantage in things like social standing, job, or education. To prevent the perpetuation of social gaps, it is crucial to make sure that human improvement technologies are available to everyone, regardless of financial status.

The repercussions of human augmentation in the long run are another ethical issue. Comprehensive scientific investigation and monitoring are required to evaluate the effectiveness, safety, and possible adverse effects of particular improvements since their full effects may not be immediately obvious. Unintended repercussions might also occur, which could have an impact on people individually as well as society as a whole. For instance, accidental genetic changes brought on by enhancement treatments may have unanticipated effects on subsequent generations.

The ethics of informed consent and autonomy should also be considered in the context for human improvement.

Individuals must be allowed the autonomy to choose whether or not to undertake therapies for betterment of their own bodies and brains. When taking into account developing technologies that require more invasive or irreversible operations, informed consent becomes more important. People should be given all the information, openness, and protections they need to properly appreciate the risks and possible advantages of the improvements they want.

Consideration of the effects of human improvement on the larger society and the environment is crucially influenced by bioethics. Improvements that are largely geared toward personal advantage should not be made at the expense of the welfare of others or the environment. For instance, the use of performance-enhancing drugs in sports to achieve physical improvements raises questions about fairness, ethics, and the possible health dangers for players. Principles that take into account the well-being of the community and the preservation of ecosystems must govern the appropriate use of enhancing technologies.

A strong regulatory framework that addresses ethical issues must be established as human enhancement technologies develop further. To create rules and laws that strike a balance between the potential advantages of human enhancement and the preservation of individual rights, social well-being, and ethical concerns, policymakers, scientists, ethicists, and the general public must work together. Safety requirements, equal access, monitoring of long-term consequences, and channels for public participation and discourse should all be parts of a complete regulatory structure.

The potential for pushing the limits of human capability, enhancing quality of life, and resolving restrictions is enormous. To navigate this complicated sector ethically, nevertheless, ethical concerns are essential. We may direct the creation and use of human enhancement technologies in a way that is consistent with our shared values and ambitions by considering issues of justice, autonomy, safety, social effect, human dignity, and the natural order. To guarantee that human enhancement makes a positive contribution to a more just, ethical, and sustainable future, it is essential to use an open-minded, interdisciplinary approach that takes into account scientific, philosophical, sociological, and regulatory viewpoints.

7.5 Sustainability and Environmental Impact

In the modern world, when it is increasingly clear that our planet must be preserved for future generations, sustainability and environmental effect are crucial ideas. In order to fulfill our current requirements while preserving the capacity of future generations to meet their own needs, sustainability refers to the prudent and balanced use of resources. On the other side, environmental impact describes the influence that human activities have on the environment, such as the exhaustion of natural resources, pollution, and climate change.

The depletion of natural resources is one of the most important problems we are now facing. Due to our present consumption habits, which are fueled by population expansion and growing industrialisation, limited resources like fossil fuels, minerals, and forests have been overused. In addition to endangering the availability of these resources for future generations, this depletion disturbs fragile ecosystems and adds to the loss of biodiversity. Sustainable methods seek to enhance resource efficiency, lessen waste production, and provide renewable substitutes in order to solve this problem.

Another big environmental consequence brought on by human activity is pollution. Pollutants are released into the air, water, and soil via industrial activities, transportation, and agriculture, which has a negative impact on ecosystems and human health. Climate change and respiratory illnesses are both exacerbated by air pollution, which is mostly caused by the combustion of fossil fuels. Water bodies get contaminated by water pollution, which is often brought on by industrial discharges and agricultural runoff. This harms aquatic life and puts human health at risk. The fertility of the soil has an influence on agriculture and biodiversity. In order to reduce pollution and safeguard the environment, sustainable methods stress the use of clean technology, waste management techniques, and stronger laws.

One of the biggest environmental problems we now face is climate change, which is mostly caused by greenhouse gas emissions. When fossil fuels are used for transportation, energy generation, and industrial activities, carbon dioxide and other greenhouse gases are released into the atmosphere. These gases trap heat, which causes a slow increase in global temperatures and has a number of negative repercussions. The effects of climate change on both natural and human systems include increased frequency and intensity of natural catastrophes, increasing sea levels, changing rainfall patterns, and changes in ecosystems. Adopting sustainable agricultural methods, encouraging reforestation, switching to renewable energy sources, and improving energy efficiency are all part of sustainable measures to combat climate change.

Another important component of environmental effect is biodiversity loss. Global biodiversity has been severely diminished by human actions including habitat loss, pollution, and deforestation. Our planet's beauty and resilience are diminished by the loss of species, and important ecological functions and services are also disrupted. By safeguarding natural ecosystems, developing sustainable land and resource management, and raising knowledge and respect for the value of biodiversity, sustainable practices seek to maintain biodiversity.

It is crucial to incorporate these concepts into all facets of society in order to achieve sustainability and reduce environmental impact. This involves environmentally friendly urban planning, in which cities are created with green areas, effective transit networks, and sustainable infrastructure. Reducing chemical inputs, conserving soil health, and fostering biodiversity on farms are the main goals of sustainable agricultural methods. Adopting circular economy models, lowering waste production, and giving environmental and social responsibility first priority are all examples of sustainable company strategies. Additionally, lowering our particular environmental footprint is greatly aided by sustainable consumption and lifestyle decisions including trash reduction, water and energy efficiency, and support for eco-friendly goods.

The connection between sustainability and environmental effect emphasizes the need to strike a balance between economic growth and the preservation of ecosystems, natural resources, and the health of our world as a whole. Our ability to forge a more resilient and peaceful future for ourselves and future generations depends on our adoption of sustainable practices and conscientious decision-making.

Chapter 8

Balancing Innovation and Regulation

8. Introduction

In the quickly changing world of today, striking a balance between innovation and regulation is a difficult but essential endeavor. Progress, economic expansion, and an improvement in the standard of living for both people and communities are all fueled by innovation. It encourages scientific research, technological development, and innovative responses to urgent problems. Innovation, however, often has risks and possible drawbacks that must be appropriately handled. In this situation, regulation is crucial.

Innovation flourishes in a setting that promotes risk-taking, supports experimentation, and nurtures creativity. Entrepreneurs, scientists, and innovators who push the limits of what is possible are the ones driving it. These entrepreneurs often work in highly disruptive and dynamic fields like technology, biotechnology, and artificial intelligence. They propose cutting-edge concepts, goods, and services that might completely alter industries and society.

Innovation may sometimes result in unforeseen effects. It might upend well-established sectors and conventional business methods, resulting in a downturn in the economy and the loss of jobs. It may also spark ethical questions about issues like invasions of privacy, inequity, and inappropriate use of technology. Furthermore, certain advances could be harmful to the environment, public safety, and health. For instance, concerns concerning road safety and accountability in the event of accidents are raised by the fast development of autonomous cars.

Here is where regulation comes into play. Protecting the public interest, ensuring fair competition, and managing risks connected with creative activity are the main goals of regulation. Regulations create standards, define game rules, and ensure compliance. The difficult balance between encouraging innovation and preserving social well-being is what they are trying to achieve.

Future-focused, adaptable, and proactive regulation is essential. It need to be planned to foresee and handle possible dangers and difficulties brought on by future technology. Regulating should not, however, discourage innovation or slow down development. It must be adaptable enough to take into account fresh concepts and changing business strategies. Regulations that are too onerous or out-of-date might act as a barrier to entrance, deter investment, and stifle innovation.

Regulators must take a cooperative stance in order to find the correct balance. To comprehend the possible ramifications of new technologies and advancements, they should interact with inventors, industry players, and specialists. This conversation may assist regulators in identifying possible dangers, staying up to date on the most recent developments, and creating the best regulatory frameworks.

Regulators are essential in promoting innovation. They may promote ethical innovation by offering direction, rewards, and a favorable ecology. For instance, regulatory sandboxes and pilot programs enable innovators to test their concepts in a regulated setting, assuring regulatory compliance while reducing pointless obstacles.

Additionally, cooperation between innovators and regulators may result in co-regulation and self-regulatory projects. Regulations may be adapted to handle particular hazards while leaving flexibility for experimentation and innovation by enlisting industry experts in the rule-making process. Self-regulatory systems that encourage ethical behaviour and ensure compliance with the law, such as industry standards and codes of conduct, may be used in addition to statutory rules.

International collaboration is another factor in striking a balance between innovation and regulation. Innovation has no national boundaries, and legal systems must adapt to changes occurring throughout the world. Cooperation between nations and international organizations may standardize standards, promote information exchange, and solve problems that traverse international borders. Through this collaboration, regulatory fragmentation may be avoided and a fair playing field for innovators throughout the globe can be guaranteed.

Progress, risk management, and social well-being all depend on finding the proper balance between innovation and regulation. Innovation promotes economic expansion, improves quality of life, and finds solutions to urgent problems. It also has dangers and the potential for undesirable outcomes, which must be appropriately handled. In order to safeguard the public interest, ensure fair competition, and manage the risks involved with innovation, regulation is essential. Effective regulation should encourage responsible innovation while preserving society values. It should also be proactive, adaptable, and future-focused. To create flexible and efficient regulatory frameworks, cooperation between regulators, innovators, and industry stakeholders is essential. In order to solve global issues and provide a coordinated approach to innovation and regulation, international collaboration is also crucial. Societies may embrace innovation's transformational potential while assuring its responsible and ethical application by finding the proper balance.

8.1 Regulatory Frameworks and Policy Challenges

Industries, economies, and public welfare are just a few of the components of society that are shaped and governed by regulatory frameworks and policy issues. These frameworks are intended to provide policies, criteria, and regulations that guarantee ethical behavior, safeguard the interests of stakeholders, and advance stability and advancement on the whole. But creating and putting in place efficient regulatory systems is not without its difficulties.

Finding the ideal balance between regulation and innovation is one of the main policy difficulties in regulatory systems. On the one hand, laws are required to protect the environment, public health, and safety. They aid in preventing monopolies, ensuring fair competition, and upholding the integrity of the market. However, excessive or unduly strict restrictions may inhibit innovation, hamper the expansion of businesses, and slow the advancement of the economy. It is a difficult task for legislators to strike a balance that allows for both regulatory control and entrepreneurial flexibility.

Keeping up with the fast changes in technology is another major difficulty. New technologies are developing at an unprecedented rate in the fast-paced world of today, upsetting established markets and business strategies. To properly handle these innovations, policy frameworks must be adaptable and agile. In order to keep up with the rapid advancement of technology, legislators must be educated, consult with experts, and regularly update rules. This is true whether they are dealing with artificial intelligence, blockchain, autonomous cars, or genetic engineering.

Another big problem for regulatory systems is posed by globalization. Regulations must take into consideration cross-border transactions, standardization, and international collaboration as economies grow more integrated. It may be challenging to combine local regulatory autonomy with global harmonization, however.

Different cultural, social, and economic conditions exist in several nations, necessitating specialized strategies. Policymakers have a difficult challenge at hand: creating international frameworks that take these distinctions into account while fostering world collaboration.

Another significant difficulty is ensuring accountability and transparency in regulatory regimes. Governmental agencies and regulatory organizations often create and enforce regulations, hence it is crucial to retain openness in these entities' decision-making procedures. Public trust may be damaged by a lack of openness, which can result in resistance and distrust. Similar to this, effective processes and checks and balances are needed to keep regulatory bodies responsible for their acts and guarantee they operate in the public's best interests.

Furthermore, new dangers and possible unintended effects need to be addressed through regulatory frameworks. Unexpected hazards and problems might occur when technology develop and new industries are created. For instance, worries about cybersecurity and money laundering have increased with the emergence of cryptocurrencies. To safeguard the public interest while promoting innovation, policymakers must foresee and proactively address these dangers.

Finally, regulatory systems must be flexible enough to evolve as norms and society do. Values, attitudes, and priorities change as cultures advance. For regulatory regulations to be current and successful, they must reflect these developments. To stay up with social expectations and make sure that the regulatory frameworks represent the general requirements and aspirations of the populace, policymakers must continually assess and update legislation.

Regulatory frameworks and policy issues are complicated and intertwined. Some of the main issues encountered by policymakers include striking a balance between regulation and innovation, keeping up with technology improvements, tackling globalization, maintaining openness and accountability, managing new hazards, and adjusting to social changes. Collaboration, stakeholder involvement, and a pro-active approach to regulatory policy-making are necessary to successfully navigate these hurdles. In a world that is changing quickly, regulatory frameworks may encourage justice, safeguard the public interest, and support sustainable development by successfully addressing these issues.

8.2 Intellectual Property and Innovation Incentives

The legal rights that have been given to people or organizations over their discoveries or works are known as intellectual property (IP). It includes a broad variety of intangible assets, such as trade secrets, patents, and copyrights. Intellectual property's primary goal is to promote and safeguard invention by giving artists and inventors exclusive rights to their works for a certain amount of time. These rights encourage people and companies to engage in R&D since they can profit from their work and stop others from using their ideas without their consent.

Incentives for innovation are essential for advancing social, technical, and economic development. Governments and legal systems guarantee that innovators and creators have a competitive edge in the market by giving intellectual property rights. This benefit motivates people to share their expertise, reveal their creations, and add to the body of human inventiveness. Without the right incentives, innovators could be hesitant to devote the time, money, and ingenuity necessary to creating new concepts for fear that rivals or copycats would reap the rewards of their labor.

Patents are one of the most often used types of intellectual property protection. Patents provide innovators exclusive rights to their creations, forbidding unauthorized production, use, or sale of the protected goods or methods. Patents encourage inventors to reveal their innovations to the public in return for a time of exclusivity by granting a temporary monopoly. The ability of innovators to recuperate their R&D expenditure and generate income during this exclusivity period fosters more innovation and boosts the economy.

Another essential component of intellectual property is copyright. It accords exclusive rights to writers, artists, musicians, and other creators in relation to their creative works. The creation of many cultural and creative expressions is encouraged by this protection. The capacity to control how their works are used, reproduced, distributed, and altered via copyright enables authors to monetize their works through licensing, sales, or other types of exploitation. Copyright supports a thriving creative sector, promotes the production of new works, and guarantees that a broad variety of cultural material is accessible to society by offering monetary benefits and legal protection.

Businesses must have trademarks in order to safeguard their names, logos, and brands. In order to identify one company's goods or services from those of other businesses, trademark registration grants the exclusive right to use a specific mark in commerce. Trademarks protect a company's image, goodwill, and market position by prohibiting rivals from utilizing identical marks. This protection encourages businesses to invest in creating strong brands and guarantees that customers can identify reliable goods and services and make educated decisions.

Another kind of intellectual property that is essential to encouraging innovation is trade secrets. Trade secrets are classified as secret business knowledge that gives a company a competitive edge. Examples include manufacturing procedures, formulae, client lists, and marketing tactics. Trade secrets, as opposed to patents or copyrights, depend on maintaining confidentiality rather than registration or disclosure. Businesses are encouraged to invest in R&D, innovation, and proprietary knowledge creation to acquire a competitive advantage in the market by preserving trade secrets.

In addition to these conventional methods of intellectual property protection, new fields of IP law are developing to deal with the difficulties brought on by technology breakthroughs. For instance, copyright and patents are used to protect ideas linked to software and computers, while protection of digital material, such as e-books or online media, has gained major attention. Additionally, the creation of new legal frameworks and enforcement methods has been prompted by problems with online piracy, counterfeiting, and the unlawful use of intellectual property that have arisen with the growth of the internet and digital technologies.

Intellectual property is criticized for potentially stifling innovation and limiting access to information and resources, especially in industries like healthcare where the availability of cost-effective medications or life-saving technology is crucial. They contend that the exclusive rights conferred by intellectual property may result in entrance hurdles, which would restrict competition and raise prices. Additionally, some contend that intellectual property protection unfairly favors big businesses with the financial means to deal with the legal system, whereas tiny producers or innovators may find it difficult to assert their rights or compete in the market.

For policymakers and legal systems, achieving a balance between the need for innovation incentives and the objectives of enabling access to information and fostering competition is a constant problem. Different nations have different views on intellectual property, with some favoring more stringent safeguards and protracted periods of exclusivity while others place more emphasis on flexibility, exceptions, and restrictions to promote innovation, access, and affordability.

Incentives for innovation and intellectual property go hand in hand. Intellectual property protection fosters innovation, propels economic progress, and promotes the creation and distribution of creative works by giving exclusive rights to inventors and creators. Research, development, and investment are strongly influenced by the use of patents, copyrights, trademarks, and trade secrets in a variety of businesses. Finding the ideal balance between encouraging innovation and fostering access to information, however, is still a challenging endeavor that need constant examination, adaptation, and taking social requirements, technical improvements, and global concerns into account.

8.3 Antitrust and Tech Monopolies

As technology corporations have grown to dominate numerous economic sectors, antitrust laws and the problem of digital monopolies have gained more attention in recent years. Antitrust laws are created to encourage healthy competition and avoid the concentration of market power in the hands of a small number of powerful competitors. However, there are worries about the possibility of monopolistic conduct on the part of internet companies like Google, Amazon, Facebook, and Apple given their fast rise and prominence.

When a single corporation or a small number of companies dominate a large amount of a certain market or sector, this is referred to as a "tech monopoly." These businesses often have strong market positions that give them the ability to control terms, establish pricing, and reshape the marketplace. The customer, rival companies, and innovation may all suffer from this power concentration.

The possibility of anti-competitive behavior with IT monopolies is one of the main issues. Predatory pricing is one of these tactics, in which a market leader cuts prices to force rivals from the market. Once the rivals are gone, the dominant business may increase prices without worrying about losing clients. Exclusive agreements, tie-ups, and discriminatory measures that prevent smaller competitors from competing fairly are some other anti-competitive actions.

Concerns about data security and privacy have also increased with the emergence of digital monopolies. These businesses often gather enormous volumes of user data, which offers them valuable market insights and a competitive edge. The ownership of such data may put prospective rivals at a disadvantage since they may not have access to the same resources. Furthermore, these businesses' possible abuse or improper management of user data may result in privacy violations and worries about the security of personal information.

Antitrust authorities are essential in guaranteeing fair competition and avoiding the exploitation of market dominance. However, it might be difficult to enforce antitrust rules in the case of technological monopolies.

Traditional antitrust laws may find it difficult to keep up with the fast development of technology and the distinctive business models used by IT firms. Due to the cross-border operations of businesses in the technology sector, it is challenging to consistently implement rules.

Policymakers and regulators have been investigating different strategies to solve these issues. Some demand for the severing of giant tech businesses to foster competition and for the tighter implementation of current antitrust laws. Others suggest updating and reforming the regulatory framework to better reflect the unique dynamics of the digital economy. Increased accountability and openness for data collection and use, standards for interoperability to promote competition, and limitations on acquisitions that can further concentrate market dominance may all be part of these changes.

Global antitrust monitoring of digital monopolies has increased in recent years. Tech businesses have been the subject of investigations and penalties by regulatory agencies in the US, the EU, and other countries for suspected antitrust infractions. Tech oligarchies have sometimes been sued and criticized by the public for their tactics and market domination. These initiatives reveal a growing understanding of the need to address the particular problems brought on by tech monopolies.

Although there are many different viewpoints on the best remedies, the problem of technological monopolies continues to be complicated. By lowering economies of scale, critics contend that dissolving tech businesses may hinder innovation and hurt consumers. They argue that rather than anti-competitive activity, market dominance results from better goods and services. On the other side, proponents of tighter antitrust laws stress the significance of maintaining competition and avoiding the concentration of power that may hinder innovation and restrict consumer choice.

The function of antitrust laws in the digital era has been hotly debated in light of the emergence of tech monopolies. Concerns regarding anti-competitive behavior, data privacy, and innovation are brought up by the concentration of market power in a small number of major IT corporations. The difficulty is in modifying the current antitrust frameworks to take into account the particular dynamics of the digital economy. In order to shape the future of the technology sector and its effects on society, it will be essential to strike the correct balance between encouraging innovation and guaranteeing fair competition.

8.4 Ethical Guidelines for Technology Development

The creation of new technologies has the potential to result in major advantages and breakthroughs across a variety of industries in the fast evolving technology environment of today. This power carries a heavy burden, however. In order to ensure that technological breakthroughs are consistent with moral principles, uphold basic rights, and benefit both the welfare of the individual and society as a whole. Transparency, privacy, justice, responsibility, and inclusion are just a few of the important ethical principles for technology development that will be covered in this paragraph.

The notion of transparency is crucial in the development of technology. It highlights the significance of open communication on the function, possible benefits, and hazards connected to a certain technology. To encourage informed decision-making, developers should work to make accurate and easily accessible information available to users and stakeholders. To prevent false or damaging results, transparency also entails disclosing any biases or technological limits.

Another crucial component of developing ethical technology is privacy. The gathering and processing of personal data has proliferated as technology becomes more widespread in our everyday lives. Developers are required to place a high priority on user privacy and make sure that personal data is handled securely, with clear permission and suitable protections. To prevent unwanted access to or exploitation of personal data, it is important to develop transparent data protection policies and strong encryption technologies.

Fairness is a value that tackles the possibility of prejudice and discrimination in the creation of technology. If not carefully built and verified, algorithms and AI systems have the potential to reinforce current biases or introduce new ones. By forming diverse and inclusive development teams, taking into account a variety of viewpoints, and routinely examining and auditing algorithms for fairness, developers should work to reduce prejudice. Equal access and opportunity are also parts of fairness, which prevents technology from escalating already-existing societal inequities.

Accountability is a key idea that makes technology creators accountable for the effects of their work. In order to detect and reduce any risks and damages related to their goods, developers should be proactive. This entails carrying out exhaustive risk analyses, requesting external audits, and setting up channels for criticism and redress. Developers should be prepared to make amends when damage is done and draw lessons from their errors to avoid repeating them in the future.

No of their origins or skills, everyone should be able to use and benefit from technology, according to the guiding concept of inclusivity. The demands of different user groups should be taken into account while designing intuitive, accessible, and inclusive technology. This entails offering different interfaces for people with disabilities, taking into account linguistic and cultural variations, and avoiding discriminatory behaviors that can further marginalize certain populations.

In order to stay up with changing society values and concerns, ethical rules for technological development also call for constant assessment and adaptation. To understand the requirements, expectations, and concerns of stakeholders, such as users, legislators, and civil society groups, developers should actively interact with them. In order to detect and resolve any unintended repercussions or possible hazards related with the technology, routine ethical assessments and impact evaluations should be carried out.

Technology improvements must adhere to ethical principles in order to be consistent with human values, uphold basic rights, and progress both individual and societal well-being. Key values that drive the development of ethical technology include transparency, privacy, justice, responsibility, and inclusion. Developers may produce technologies that have a good effect, improve people's lives, and contribute to a more just and sustainable future by abiding by these principles.

8.5 Public-Private Partnerships for Technological Advancement

Public-private partnerships (PPPs) have become a potent tool for promoting innovation and accelerating development across a range of industries. In order to tackle difficult problems and realize the promise of new technologies, this collaborative strategy combines the talents and resources of the public and private sectors. PPPs promote rapid development, implementation, and spread of technology solutions by using their complementary knowledge, resulting in social advantages and economic progress.

PPPs work on the basis of cooperation, with the public and private sectors coming together to define shared objectives and pool resources to accomplish them. These collaborations often center on R&D, infrastructure development, and the use of cutting-edge technology to solve urgent problems in the context of technological progress. Governments offer the required funds, access to public resources, and regulatory frameworks, whilst private businesses provide their sector experience, technological know-how, and financial investments.

The potential of PPPs to close the gap between research and commercialization is one of their main advantages. These collaborations promote cooperation between academics, research facilities, and private businesses, which makes it easier to translate scientific findings into usable applications and marketable goods. PPPs encourage the development of cutting-edge technologies that have the potential to reshape sectors and enhance quality of life, such as artificial intelligence, biotechnology, renewable energy, and advanced manufacturing.

PPPs for technical progress can promote capacity building and information exchange. They encourage communication between public and private parties to share knowledge, best practices, and technological know-how. This idea and skill exchange speeds up learning and contributes to the development of a trained workforce that can propel technological innovation. Additionally, it promotes the diffusion of technical developments across industries and geographical areas, which aids in inclusive growth and bridges the digital divide.

PPPs are essential to the development of infrastructure, in addition to research and development. Governments may close the substantial financial gap for developing and updating vital infrastructure by using private sector contributions. PPPs allow for the integration of cutting-edge technology and guarantee effective and sustainable infrastructure solutions, whether they be for telecommunications networks, transportation systems, or smart cities. These collaborations rely on the effectiveness, creativity, and risk-sharing of the private sector to execute projects more successfully, on schedule, and under budget.

PPPs for technology development encourage entrepreneurship and aid the expansion of start-ups and small and medium-sized companies (SMEs). These collaborations foster an atmosphere that is conducive to the success of innovation-driven businesses by giving them access to resources including funding, mentoring, and market possibilities. Large organizations acquire new views and access to innovative technology, while startups profit from the know-how and networks of well-established businesses. This interaction between SMEs, startups, and established companies cultivates a dynamic ecosystem that supports both economic expansion and technical innovation.

PPPs for technical progress do not, however, come without difficulties. It might be challenging to strike a balance between the expectations and interests of public and private partners. Priorities, risk tolerances, and schedules may diverge, necessitating the use of competent negotiation, communication, and conflict resolution techniques. Moreover, sustaining public confidence and preserving the PPPs' long-term viability require assuring transparency, accountability, and equal benefit sharing.

Technology-related public-private partnerships are effective engines for advancing innovation, solving social issues, and promoting economic development. These collaborations take use of the resources, know-how, and networks available via the public and commercial sectors to hasten the creation and application of technology solutions. PPPs leverage the promise of new technologies and assist equitable and sustainable development via infrastructure development, research and development, and entrepreneurship support. To overcome obstacles and reap the advantages of these joint endeavors, however, proper planning, efficient administration, and a unified vision are needed.

Chapter 9

The Future of Technopolitics

9. Introduction

As we continue to see the fast growth of technology and its effects on political institutions and administration, the future of technopolitics is a subject of enormous concern and speculative interest. The term "technopolitics" describes the nexus between technology and politics, where advancements in technology have an impact on political systems, power relationships, and decision-making. It seems obvious that technopolitics will have a growing impact on how societies and political systems throughout the globe are shaped as time goes on.

The development of social media and digital platforms as potent instruments for political involvement and mobilization is one of the essential elements of the future of technopolitics. We have seen firsthand how powerfully social media sites like Facebook, Twitter, and YouTube have influenced public opinion, facilitated political conversation, and sparked large-scale movements during the last ten years. These platforms have given people unparalleled access to information, allowing them to voice their opinions, plan demonstrations, and shape public policy. Thoughts have also been expressed about algorithmic bias, false information, and the consolidation of power in the hands of a few number of tech companies as a result of the growth of digital platforms. In the future, an important component of technopolitical administration will be achieving a balance between the advantages and difficulties offered by these platforms.

The future of technopolitics will also be significantly impacted by developing technologies like artificial intelligence (AI), blockchain, and the Internet of Things (IoT). With its capacity to analyze enormous quantities of data and generate predictions, AI has the potential to completely transform how governments make decisions. AI systems are capable of assessing policy alternatives and forecasting the results of legislative initiatives, giving policymakers useful information. To guarantee that AI is responsibly incorporated into political processes, concerns about transparency, accountability, and ethical usage must be resolved.

On the other side, blockchain technology has the potential to increase political process security, trust, and transparency. Blockchain enables safe voting systems, streamlines bureaucratic processes, and eradicates corruption by offering decentralized and immutable ledgers. Government may become more effective and transparent by using blockchain-based solutions in areas like campaign funding, public procurement, and identity verification. To reach its full potential in the field of technopolitics, blockchain must overcome the difficulties of scalability, interoperability, and regulatory frameworks.

Additionally, when Internet of Things (IoT) devices proliferate, massive quantities of data will be produced, which may be used to support evidence-based policy choices. IoT sensors in smart cities may give real-time data on energy use, environmental conditions, and traffic patterns, allowing planners to create more sustainable and effective urban settings. However, the gathering and analysis of this data raises issues related to surveillance, data security, and privacy. The future of technopolitics will be shaped by finding a balance between the advantages of IoT-driven policy solutions and protecting individual liberties.

The increased interaction between governments and private tech corporations will have an impact on technopolitics in the future, in addition to these technical developments. Public-private collaborations have the potential to spur innovation, provide effective public services, and stimulate the economy. This partnership also prompts questions about monopolistic behavior, the deterioration of democratic standards, and the impact of corporate interests on public policy. Navigating the future of technopolitics will need the development of strong governance mechanisms to control these collaborations, maintain transparency, and avoid the misuse of power.

Future developments in technopolitics have the potential to significantly alter political and governmental institutions. The emergence of digital platforms, the incorporation of cutting-edge technology, and the cooperation between governments and tech firms will influence political processes, power structures, and decision-making. To take advantage of technopolitics' advantages while resolving its problems, it is critical that politicians, technologists, and people have intelligent dialogues, create ethical frameworks, and develop inclusive governance models. By doing this, we can sculpt a future in which politics and technology collaborate to build societies that are more open, inclusive, and responsible.

9.1 Emerging Technologies and Trends

The way we live, work, and interact with the world around us is revolutionized by new technologies and trends, which are also influencing the future of many businesses. Numerous technologies, including artificial intelligence (AI), blockchain, the internet of things (IoT), virtual reality (VR), and renewable energy, have made significant strides in recent years. These technologies are spurring innovation, opening up new possibilities, and tackling difficult problems in previously unheard-of ways.

With applications ranging from machine learning algorithms that can handle enormous quantities of data and make intelligent judgments to natural language processing systems that allow human-like interactions, artificial intelligence has emerged as a disruptive technology. Healthcare, banking, manufacturing, and transportation are just a few of the industries that are using AI to increase production, efficiency, and accuracy while laying the groundwork for self-driving cars and intelligent automation.

Blockchain technology has developed into a potent tool for safe and decentralized transactions after being first popularized by cryptocurrencies like Bitcoin. Its distributed ledger mechanism assures transparency, immutability, and trust while doing away with the need for middlemen. Beyond financial transactions, blockchain technology is being investigated for use in voting systems, healthcare records, supply chain management, and intellectual property rights. It offers enhanced security, efficiency, and accountability.

The Internet of Things has expanded significantly, providing easy connection and data sharing by connecting commonplace gadgets and things to the internet. The growth of smart homes, smart cities, and industrial automation is being driven by this integrated network of physical devices, sensors, and software. The Internet of Things (IoT) has the potential to improve convenience, optimize resource allocation, and allow predictive maintenance, but it also raises issues with data management, privacy, and security.

The way we interact with and consume digital material is changing as a result of virtual reality and augmented reality technology. AR projects digital information over the actual world, but VR builds virtual worlds that are fully immersive. These technologies provide realistic and engaging experiences in gaming, education, healthcare, and training simulations. VR and AR are set to change entertainment, communication, and numerous professional fields as the gear becomes more accessible and inexpensive.

Technologies for renewable energy are becoming more and more crucial in light of climate change and the need to cut greenhouse gas emissions. The use of solar, wind, and hydropower is expanding because to developments in energy storage, grid integration, and efficiency. The development of a sustainable and robust energy sector is fueled by the switch to clean energy sources, which also provides advantages for the environment, energy security, and economic prospects.

In order to reduce latency and bandwidth needs, edge computing involves processing and analyzing data closer to its source. Edge computing is becoming more and more popular due to the growth of IoT devices and the need for real-time analytics. Particularly in distant or resource-constrained contexts, it provides quicker decision-making, enhanced security, and cost-effective data administration.

By opening up new options in illness treatment, medication research, and agricultural enhancement, biotechnology and genetic engineering are changing healthcare and agriculture. The development of gene editing methods like CRISPR has made it possible to modify genetic material precisely, perhaps curing hereditary diseases and improving agricultural yields. However, since these technologies have complicated ethical and societal ramifications, ethical issues and regulatory frameworks are essential.

Our world is changing as a result of new trends and technology, which are also spurring innovation in several industries. The revolutionary technologies that are reshaping industries and having an influence on our everyday lives include AI, blockchain, IoT, VR/AR, renewable energy, edge computing, and biotechnology. Although there is great promise for development, efficiency, and sustainability, these technologies also present issues with privacy, legislation, and ethics. Given the potential long-term social effects of these technologies, it is crucial to promote their responsible development and implementation.

9.2 Democratizing Technological Access

Technology has permeated every aspect of our everyday lives in the quickly evolving digital era of today. It has changed the way we interact with one another, do business, study, and simply pass the time. The digital gap occurs between those who have access to technology and those who do not, despite the many advantages it provides. This discrepancy in access to technology, which is often driven by elements like socioeconomic position, location, and education, presents substantial difficulties and impedes the advancement of both people and society. The idea of democratizing technical access has become a potent force promoting inclusive development, empowerment, and equitable development in response to this urgent challenge.

Fundamentally, democratizing technical access means giving everyone the chance to access technology's revolutionary potential, regardless of their circumstances or background. It aims to close the digital gap and get rid of obstacles that impede people and communities from taking use of new technology. By democratizing access, we want to level the playing field so that everyone can access, benefit from, and contribute to technology-driven solutions.

The availability of hardware and infrastructure that is both inexpensive and accessible is one of the fundamental tenets of democratizing technology access. This entails increasing the accessibility and affordability of gadgets like cellphones, laptops, and internet connection. Governments, nonprofit groups, and businesses all play a significant part in this by putting out programs like community technology centers, free Wi-Fi networks, and device subsidy schemes. People from underprivileged backgrounds may get the tools required to participate in the digital world by eliminating entrance barriers.

In addition to physical accessibility, developing digital literacy and skills is crucial for democratizing access to technology. It is not enough to just provide people access to gadgets and the internet; they also need to be given the knowledge and abilities to use technology well. Offering comprehensive digital literacy programs that encompass fundamental computer skills, internet navigation, online safety, and coding will need cooperation between educational institutions, community groups, and governmental organizations. For people from all backgrounds to improve their digital skills and take part in the digital economy, such programs should be created to appeal to all age groups and ability levels.

Additionally, democratizing technical access goes beyond individual empowerment and includes making sure that underrepresented and underprivileged groups have an equal chance to participate in and make contributions to the technology sector. Inclusion and diversity in the IT industry are essential for fostering innovation and taking into account the particular demands and viewpoints of varied groups. Scholarships, mentoring programs, and inclusive hiring practices are just a few examples of initiatives aimed at fostering diversity in technology that are crucial to removing obstacles and building a more welcoming digital industry.

Sharing information and using open-source software are also essential to democratizing access to technology. Open-source efforts allow people and groups to freely access, change, and share software by promoting a culture of cooperation and sharing. This encourages creativity and individualization and lessens reliance on proprietary technology. By enabling people to tinker, explore, and come up with their own solutions, open-source hardware initiatives, like low-cost computer platforms, democratize the means of production and creativity.

Additionally, public policies and regulatory frameworks are essential for democratizing access to technology. Governments must implement laws that enable broad internet access, uphold net neutrality, and encourage service provider competition. Regulations should also be in place to guarantee data security and privacy, stop the exploitation of personal data, and protect people's digital rights. Governments may make a big contribution to democratizing access to technology by fostering an environment that promotes innovation, competition, and the protection of user rights.

The democratization of technical access has the potential to make people throughout the world more talented, creative, and enterprising. It may promote social inclusion, encourage economic progress, and give people more control over their own lives. Technology can empower communities, end the cycle of poverty, and eliminate the socio-economic gap by giving access to educational resources, healthcare information, financial services, and other crucial tools.

However, democratizing access to technology is a continuous process that calls for cooperation from several parties. To ensure that technology becomes a catalyst for good change and empowerment, governments, civil society groups, educational institutions, commercial sector companies, and people must all play a role in removing obstacles. Together, we can build a world where no one is left behind and everyone has access to the full power of technology for both their own personal development and the advancement of society as a whole.

9.3 Redesigning Governance Systems

The process of redesigning governance systems is intricate and varied with the goal of enhancing the efficacy, accountability, and efficiency of governmental institutions. To answer the changing requirements and difficulties of societies, it entails reinventing the governance system's structure, procedures, and decision-making mechanisms. Traditional forms of government have often come under fire for being bureaucratic, inflexible, and unable to keep up with the fast changes in technology, demography, and interconnectivity of the world. A comprehensive strategy that values innovation, inclusion, openness, and public involvement is needed to redesign governance structures.

The use of technology to improve governmental operations and service delivery is a crucial component in redesigning governance systems. Initiatives including digitalization and e-governance may increase access to public services, minimize corruption, and expedite administrative procedures. Governments may improve decision-making processes, improve policy formulation, and support evidence-based governance by embracing new technologies like artificial intelligence, blockchain, and data analytics.

Redesigning governance systems entails not just incorporating new technology but also rethinking the function and organization of public institutions. More decentralized and participative forms of governance are posing a threat to conventional hierarchical institutions. Subsidiarity, a theory that favors making decisions at the lowest possible level, is gaining popularity as a way to strengthen local communities and encourage bottom-up engagement.

As part of the redesign of governance structures, a more citizen-centric mindset must be adopted. Governments are realizing the value of including the public in decision-making, encouraging openness, and setting up systems for accountability and feedback. Public discussions, participatory budgeting, and the co-creation of policies are just a few examples of the many ways that citizens may participate. Governments may guarantee that policies and services are more aligned with the needs and aspirations of the people by incorporating individuals in governance.

Furthermore, a focus on sustainability and resilience is required while revamping governance systems. Governments must embrace long-term planning and proactive actions as the globe grapples with complex issues like climate change, resource shortages, and pandemics. The Paris Agreement and other sustainable development frameworks provide a road map for incorporating environmental, social, and economic factors into governance structures. Building resilience via effective crisis management, risk assessment, and adaptable governance frameworks is also essential for navigating unpredictable and unstable times.

Fostering cooperation and collaborations among many stakeholders is another need for redesigning governance structures. Governments cannot resolve all social concerns on their own; thus, collaboration with private sector companies, academic institutions, and international organizations is crucial. Collective action toward shared objectives is made possible by collaborative governance models, which encourage shared decision-making, resource sharing, and knowledge exchange.

Redesigning governance structures also requires a dedication to honesty and ethical leadership. Combating corruption, fostering accountability, and upholding the rule of law must be given top priority by governments. Building trust between the government and its constituents via transparent and accountable governance systems promotes social cohesion and sustainable development.

A dynamic and continuing process called governance system redesign aims to modernize established forms of government to better serve the demands of the twenty-first century. It entails using technology, giving authority to the people, embracing sustainability, encouraging teamwork, and preserving moral principles. Governments may establish more effective, responsive, and inclusive governance systems that meet the complex issues of our day by adopting these principles and putting creative ideas into practice.

9.4 Human-Centered Technopolitics

A concept known as "human-centered technopolitics" unites the fields of technology and politics with a focus on putting people at the center of decision-making. It recognizes that technology has a huge influence on society and works to ensure that technical improvements are in line with people's values, needs, and ambitions.

Human-Centered Technopolitics is fundamentally aware that technology is not value-neutral. It recognises the significant social, economic, and ethical ramifications that the creation and use of technology may have. In order to promote human well-being, equality, and justice, it thus calls for an inclusive and participatory approach to developing and controlling technology systems.

In Human-Centered Technopolitics, the significance of enabling people and communities to actively participate in technological decision-making processes is emphasized. This entails making information accessible, promoting digital literacy, and establishing forums for public discussion and debate. It aims to avoid the concentration of power and advance inclusion, diversity, and representation by incorporating a range of stakeholders in the decision-making process.

The understanding of the interaction between technical advancement and larger political, economic, and social systems is another important component of human-centered technopolitics. It recognizes that advancing technology is inextricably entwined with current power dynamics and structural inequities rather than operating in a vacuum. In order to avoid maintaining or escalating inequities, it aims to address these fundamental problems and utilize technology to undermine and modify current power systems.

The concept of using technology as a tool for group action and social change is also promoted by human-centered technopolitics. It acknowledges that technology has the ability to empower people and groups to organize, mobilize, and express their concerns, promoting a more democratic and participatory society. It promotes open and accountable governance systems where choices about technology are exposed to inspection.

9.5 Collaborative Governance and Co-creation

Due to their potential to promote efficient problem-solving, creativity, and inclusive decision-making processes, collaborative governance and co-creation are two ideas that have attracted a lot of attention in recent years. In order to collectively address complex societal challenges and make decisions that reflect a diversity of perspectives and interests, various stakeholders, including government entities, private organizations, civil society groups, and individuals, work together in collaborative governance. It stresses the value of teamwork, cooperation, and shared accountability in developing public policy and putting forth practical solutions.

Power dynamics are more evenly distributed and decision-making procedures are inclusive, open, and participatory under collaborative governance. It acknowledges that many stakeholders each contribute different information, experiences, and resources to the table, allowing for a comprehensive comprehension of the issue at hand. Collaborative governance aims to develop creative thinking, mutual trust and understanding, and a feeling of ownership among stakeholders by using this variety. This method permits the creation of long-term, contextually relevant solutions that are more likely to gain acceptance and be successfully implemented.

The process of collaboratively generating value, solutions, or experiences via the active engagement and cooperation of many stakeholders is the emphasis of co-creation, on the other hand. It entails removing long-standing barriers between producers and customers, beneficiaries and experts, and it promotes open communication and participation throughout the innovation and decision-making processes. The idea behind co-creation is that by integrating stakeholders in the development and delivery of policies, programs, or services, more relevant and user-centered results may be produced.

In order to build a thorough knowledge of the needs and goals of all stakeholders, co-creation places a strong emphasis on the value of empathy, active listening, and constant communication. It entails a transition from a top-down to a bottom-up strategy that is more participative and incorporates stakeholders in issue description, idea formulation, prototyping, and assessment. Co-creation makes stakeholders active participants and co-owners of the solutions, which boosts happiness, trust, and the possibility that results will be successful.

Co-creation and collaborative governance both call for a change in corporate culture and philosophy. They oppose conventional hierarchical systems and promote cooperation, adaptation, and flexibility. They also call for the creation of brand-new platforms and processes that promote communication, information exchange, and group decision-making. By offering tools and platforms for communication, collaboration, and information sharing, technology is a key factor in allowing collaborative governance and co-creation.

Numerous domains, including urban planning, public policy, healthcare, environmental management, and social innovation, have effectively used collaborative governance and co-creation. By using the pooled knowledge, ingenuity, and resources of many stakeholders, these techniques have shown to be successful in solving difficult and systemic concerns, such as reducing poverty, combating climate change, and addressing social injustice.

Co-creation and collaborative governance, however, are not without difficulties, and this must be understood. All parties involved must invest the necessary time, money, and effort. These strategies' efficacy may be hampered by power disparities, competing interests, and low levels of cooperation. Creating a culture of collaboration and co-creation, guaranteeing diversity, and fostering trust are continual activities that call for constant work and care.

Co-creation and collaborative governance provide potential ways to handle complicated social problems and promote inclusive decision-making. These strategies may result in more inventive, context-specific, and sustainable solutions by including many stakeholders, using their special knowledge and skills, and promoting teamwork. While obstacles remain, collaborative governance and co-creation are useful approaches for addressing the complex issues of our day and constructing more inclusive and resilient communities, notwithstanding any possible drawbacks.

Chapter 10

Conclusion

A broad notion called "technopolitics" examines the complex interrelationship between politics and technology in modern society. We have examined several facets of technopolitics in this discussion, illuminating its effects on power structures, government, and the democratization of knowledge. The emergence of cutting-edge technology has altered the political environment by opening up new channels for communication, monitoring, and control. We have seen the development of online communities that support political action and mobilization, as well as the growing importance of data-driven decision-making in the formulation of public policy. This change is not without difficulties, however. Privacy issues, algorithmic prejudice, and the consolidation of power in the hands of digital corporations are issues that need to be addressed immediately. We have now completed our analysis of technopolitics, and it is clear that more research and discussion are needed. We can traverse the complexity of technopolitics and harness its promise for societal improvement by embracing technical breakthroughs responsibly, promoting diversity, and defending democratic ideals.

In summary, technopolitics is a powerful and transforming force in the globe today. Politics and technology interact in a complex way, creating both previously unimaginable possibilities and difficulties. On the one hand, the spread of digital technology has given people and groups more power, enabling them to participate in politics, plan social movements, and question established power structures. In order to keep governments responsible and take part in decision-making processes, the internet and social media platforms have permitted the quick distribution of information. Furthermore, developments in data analytics and artificial intelligence may improve service provision and policy development, increasing governance's efficacy and efficiency.

Technopolitics does have its drawbacks, however. Concerns about privacy, monitoring, and the deterioration of civil rights have arisen as a result of the ubiquitous impact of technology in our lives. Massive quantities of personal data are being collected and analyzed, which raises concerns about security, consent, and the possibility of abuse or exploitation by both state- and non-state actors. Concerns about algorithmic bias, filter bubbles, and power concentration are brought up by the dominance of IT firms and their algorithms. Furthermore, the transmission of false information has been accelerated and magnified online, weakening the basic underpinnings of democratic dialogue.

It is crucial that politicians, technologists, and people participate in a critical and continuing discussion in order to manage the complexity of technopolitics. In order to maximize the benefits of technology while minimizing its perils, it is essential to preserve individuals' private rights, ensure data security, and enact strict rules. To allow people to critically analyze information and efficiently navigate the digital world, it is crucial to promote media literacy and digital literacy. Additionally, it is crucial to promote inclusion and close the digital gap to guarantee fair access to technology and avoid escalating already-existing socio-economic imbalances.

Technopolitics' destiny ultimately rests on our collective hands. We can create a technopolitical environment that benefits everyone by embracing technology breakthroughs responsibly, fostering a culture of openness and responsibility, and supporting democratic norms. We can unlock the enormous potential of technopolitics for the advancement of society as a whole only via a conscientious and educated engagement with technology, together with a dedication to upholding individual rights and democratic ideals.

References

1. Floridi, L. (2019). The Logic of Information: A Theory of Philosophy as Conceptual Design. Oxford University Press.

2. Graham, S., & Marvin, S. (2001). Splintering Urbanism: Networked Infrastructures, Technological Mobilities and the Urban Condition. Routledge.

3. Hague, R., & Loader, B. D. (Eds.). (2019). Digital Citizenship: The Internet, Society, and Participation. Routledge.

4. Harari, Y. N. (2018). 21 Lessons for the 21st Century. Spiegel & Grau.

5. Himma, K. E., & Tavani, H. T. (Eds.). (2008). The Handbook of Information and Computer Ethics. John Wiley & Sons.

6. Nye, J. S. (2017). The Future of Power. PublicAffairs.

7. O'Brien, D. Z., & Williams, A. M. (Eds.). (2020). Internet Politics: States, Citizens, and New Communication Technologies. Oxford University Press.

8. Pariser, E. (2011). The Filter Bubble: What the Internet Is Hiding from You. Penguin.

9. Pasquale, F. (2015). The Black Box Society: The Secret Algorithms That Control Money and Information. Harvard University Press.

10. Rose, N. (1999). Powers of Freedom: Reframing Political Thought. Cambridge University Press.

11. Sassen, S. (2014). Expulsions: Brutality and Complexity in the Global Economy. Harvard University Press.

12. Van Dijk, J. A. (2012). The Network Society (3rd ed.). Sage Publications.

13. Castells, M. (2010). The Rise of the Network Society (2nd ed.). Wiley-Blackwell.

14. Cohen, J. E. (2019). Between Truth and Power: The Legal Constructions of Informational Capitalism. Oxford University Press.

15. Floridi, L. (2014). The Fourth Revolution: How the Infosphere Is Reshaping Human Reality. Oxford University Press.

16. Morozov, E. (2013). To Save Everything, Click Here: The Folly of Technological Solutionism. PublicAffairs.

17. Norris, P. (2001). Digital Divide: Civic Engagement, Information Poverty, and the Internet Worldwide. Cambridge University Press.

18. Rheingold, H. (2002). Smart Mobs: The Next Social Revolution. Basic Books.

19. Taylor, A. S., & Floridi, L. (Eds.). (2017). The Routledge Handbook of Philosophy of Information. Routledge.

20. Tufekci, Z. (2017). Twitter and Tear Gas: The Power and Fragility of Networked Protest. Yale University Press.

21. Winner, L. (1997). The Whale and the Reactor: A Search for Limits in an Age of High Technology. University of Chicago Press.

22. Zuboff, S. (2019). The Age of Surveillance Capitalism: The Fight for a Human Future at the New Frontier of Power. PublicAffairs.

23. Bratton, B. H. (2016). The Stack: On Software and Sovereignty. MIT Press.

24. Fuchs, C. (2014). Digital Labour and Karl Marx. Routledge.

25. Coleman, G. E. (2013). Coding Freedom: The Ethics and Aesthetics of Hacking. Princeton University Press.

26. O'Neil, C. (2016). Weapons of Math Destruction: How Big Data Increases Inequality and Threatens Democracy. Broadway Books.

27. Zuboff, S. (1988). In the Age of the Smart Machine: The Future of Work and Power. Basic Books.

28. Srnicek, N. (2017). Platform Capitalism. Polity Press.

29. Zuboff, S. (2003). The Support Economy: Why Corporations Are Failing Individuals and the Next Episode of Capitalism. Penguin.

30. Graham, S. (2019). The Smart City in a Digital World. Routledge.